▶ **Big Data in History**

DOI: 10.1057/9781137378972

Other Palgrave Pivot titles

Mitchell Congram, Peter Bell and Mark Lauchs: Policing Transnational Organised Crime and Corruption: Exploring Communication Interception Technology

János Kelemen: The Rationalism of Georg Lukács

Susan D. Rose: Challenging Global Gender Violence: The Global Clothesline Project

Thomas Janoski: Dominant Divisions of Labor: Models of Production That Have Transformed the World of Work

Gray Read: Modern Architecture in Theater: The Experiments of Art et Action

Robert Frodeman: Sustainable Knowledge: A Theory of Interdisciplinarity

Antonio V. Menéndez Alarcón: French and US Approaches to Foreign Policy

Stephen Turner: American Sociology: From Pre-Disciplinary to Post-Normal

Ekaterina Dorodnykh: Stock Market Integration: An International Perspective

Bill Lucarelli: Endgame for the Euro: A Critical History

Mercedes Bunz: The Silent Revolution: How Digitalization Transforms Knowledge, Work, Journalism and Politics without Making Too Much Noise

Kishan S. Rana: The Contemporary Embassy: Paths to Diplomatic Excellence

Mark Bracher: Educating for Cosmopolitanism: Lessons from Cognitive Science and Literature

Carroll P. Kakel, III: The Holocaust as Colonial Genocide: Hitler's 'Indian Wars' in the 'Wild East'

Laura Linker: Lucretian Thought in Late Stuart England: Debates about the Nature of the Soul

Nicholas Birns: Barbarian Memory: The Legacy of Early Medieval History in Early Modern Literature

Adam Graycar and Tim Prenzler: Understanding and Preventing Corruption

Michael J. Pisani: Consumption, Informal Markets, and the Underground Economy: Hispanic Consumption in South Texas

Joan Marques: Courage in the Twenty-First Century

Samuel Tobin: Portable Play in Everyday Life: The Nintendo DS

George P. Smith: Palliative Care and End-of-Life Decisions

Majia Holmer Nadesan: Fukushima and the Privatization of Risk

Ian I. Mitroff, Lindan B. Hill, and Can M. Alpaslan: Rethinking the Education Mess: A Systems Approach to Education Reform

G. Douglas Atkins: T.S. Eliot, Lancelot Andrewes, and the Word: Intersections of Literature and Christianity

Emmeline Taylor: Surveillance Schools: Security, Discipline and Control in Contemporary Education

Daniel J. Hill and Daniel Whistler: The Right to Wear Religious Symbols

Donald Kirk: Okinawa and Jeju: Bases of Discontent

Sara Hsu: Lessons in Sustainable Development from China & Taiwan

Paola Coletti: Evidence for Public Policy Design: How to Learn from Best Practices

Thomas Paul Bonfiglio: Why Is English Literature? Language and Letters for the Twenty-First Century

DOI: 10.1057/9781137378972

palgrave▸pivot

# Big Data in History

## Patrick Manning

*Andrew Mellon Professor of World History &*
*Director, Collaborative for Historical Information and*
*Analysis, University of Pittsburgh*

palgrave
macmillan

DOI: 10.1057/9781137378972

First published 2013 by
PALGRAVE MACMILLAN

Palgrave Macmillan in the UK is an imprint of Macmillan Publishers Limited, registered in England, company number 785998, of Houndmills, Basingstoke, Hampshire RG21 6XS.

Palgrave Macmillan in the US is a division of St Martin's Press LLC, 175 Fifth Avenue, New York, NY 10010.

Palgrave Macmillan is the global academic imprint of the above companies and has companies and representatives throughout the world.

Palgrave® and Macmillan® are registered trademarks in the United States, the United Kingdom, Europe and other countries.

ISBN: 978–1–137–37898–9  EPUB
ISBN: 978–1–137–37897–2  PDF
ISBN: 978–1–137–37896–5  Hardback

A catalogue record for this book is available from the British Library.

A catalog record for this book is available from the Library of Congress.

www.palgrave.com/pivot

DOI: 10.1057/9781137378972

# Contents

# List of Illustrations

## Figures

## Table

DOI: 10.1057/9781137378972

# Preface

This little book arises out of the intensive yet widely distributed effort to create a world-historical data resource. Collaborative effort has centered particularly at the University of Pittsburgh, where the World History Center has provided an institutional base and a source of funding, and where the School of Information Science has provided administrative support, faculty research and commentary, and research by graduate students. The Dietrich School of Arts and Sciences, led by Dean N. John Cooper, created the World History Center and supported it with small grants and appointment of a post-doctoral fellow. The Office of the Provost, with particular thanks to George Klinzing, provided essential financial and moral support at a difficult juncture.

Several other universities and research institutes have been essential to confirming the international and collaborative nature of this project. The Center for Geographic Analysis and the Institute for Quantitative Social Science at Harvard University offered leadership at the start, soon followed by the International Institute of Social History in Amsterdam and the University of Portsmouth. Colleagues at Boston University, University of California – Merced, and Michigan State University then joined in, and others are to follow. The most important institutional support arrived with the 2012 award from the National Science Foundation for three years of work to build the infrastructure of the Collaborative for Historical Information and Analysis.

At an individual level, I express my appreciation to those who contributed to development of the vision that is articulated not only in this book but especially in the ongoing work of research and development. Adam McKeown joined me in the initial sketches of this work at Northeastern University, 1998–2000. In the years 2007–2008, the project gestated and established its connections with parallel groups. Siddharth Chandra became my first partner in this work at Pitt; Geoffrey Bowker provided early inspiration, while Hassan Karimi and Ron Larsen added insights and assistance. From other institutions, Peter K. Bol, Gary King, Ruth Mostern, John Gerring, Bob Woodberry, Lex Berman, Humphrey Southall, Marcel van der Linden, and Ulbe Bosma contributed their links to one after another of the parallel groups pursuing this work. From 2009 to 2011 this growing group wrote up collaborative grant applications which cemented their relationships and clarified the tasks and their explication. At Pitt, Johan Mohd Sani built the World-Historical Dataverse website and its content; Daniel Bain, Wilbert van Panhuis, and Donald Burke led in imaginative work to link health, climate, and population records; and Vladimir Zadorozhny persisted in demonstrating the key role of crowdsourcing in large datasets. From 2011, CHIA took its formal form, and within a year its first major funding had been obtained, in the form of National Science Foundation Award 1244672: the award greatly assisted the completion of this book. Kai Cao joined the research staff at Pitt and Emily Palmer performed essential administrative tasks. Then new expansion in collaboration brought ties with Jan Luiten van Zanden of CLIO-INFRA (Amsterdam), Ebrima Sall of CODESRIA (Dakar), and Pablo Gentili of CLACSO (Buenos Aires). Inevitably, other important figures are neglected in this recounting of an expanding network of scholarship.

The current stage of the CHIA project is to build infrastructure – the archive and the system for data ingest and documentation. Yet the most important element of the infrastructure, as we are learning, is the human system of collaboration – the willingness to collaborate, share, provide frank commentary, and to meet deadlines. We have made some progress and look forward to further advances. It has been my great pleasure to attempt to coordinate so many of the pieces of this big project. The errors in this overview are my own, but I expect my colleagues to speak up quickly and make the necessary corrections.

This work is dedicated to the historians at all levels who are collecting information on the human past. It is dedicated as well to the audience of researchers, teachers, and students who will – if all goes well – be able to explore world history through the resource of the public archive that will result from this project.

DOI: 10.1057/9781137378972

# 1

# Challenges of Big Data in History

Abstract: *This book makes the case for expanding the worldwide historical archive now under development through the Collaborative for Historical Information and Analysis (CHIA). The opening chapter emphasizes that the time has come for using available technology to create a coherent record of human social change in recent centuries, so as to link patterns of past change to the great policy decisions our society faces. The chapter underscores the fundamentally collaborative nature of CHIA's expanding worldwide project, comparing it to existing projects in climate modeling and genetic databases. It describes the five major levels of the archive – tied together by the three missions for developing them – and the global analysis that will emerge from the fifth level. It introduces the succeeding chapters on the construction of the global historical archive and its intended use by researchers and the general public.*

Keywords: collaborative; social change

Manning, Patrick. *Big Data in History*. Basingstoke: Palgrave Macmillan, 2013. DOI: 10.1057/9781137378972.

# The time has come: meeting the challenge

The time has come for creating and analyzing a global dataset on human societal activities. Such a dataset can provide a picture of worldwide social patterns and interactions over the past four or more centuries. Basically, this world-historical dataset is to portray long-term, global change in human society and thereby provide a basis for planning long-term, global policies for the future. Often, plans have been made for the future with little idea of the dynamics inherited from the past and little sense of the directions in which those dynamics are restructuring the present. And while the past is both known and forgotten at local and national levels, at the global level we have almost no knowledge of the historical forces and experiences that have unfolded within human society.

The organization of Big Data in history will provide a new, comprehensive level of documentation on the past. Currently available historical information, while enormous in its overall quantity, lies scattered and dispersed among many repositories. Libraries and archives in great cities hold treasure troves of data on trade, politics, and religion for national and imperial centers, but each archive is separate from the other, and the totality of their records provides rather scanty information on the numerous people in the rural areas.[1] The idea of Big Data in history is to digitize a growing portion of existing historical documentation, to link the scattered records to each other (by place, time, and topic), and to create a comprehensive picture of the various changes in human society over the past four or five centuries. This volume provides an overview indicating the types of historical data to be assembled, the techniques for storing and analyzing these records, and the type of patterns and connections in local histories and world history that could come from creation of this global dataset. Initial stages of the global dataset focus on evidence about the economy, society, politics, health and climate. Later on, the project will address Big Data on ideas, culture, and values.

The challenge is huge: there are great quantities of data to be collected and processed, and the work of processing will be complex. Big Data in history is not like the data harvested from mobile phones or commercial records. Today's phone and other data are consistent in format because they are born digital, including straightforward metadata to describe the data. Instead, historical data mostly exist in small files that need to be digitized, documented, and transformed to become parallel to other

DOI: 10.1057/9781137378972

datasets before they can be analyzed. The cost of collecting and archiving historical data is therefore much higher than for contemporary data.

But if the cost of historical data is great, the value is even greater. Most basically, data from the past can give us insight into change over time, a factor addressed only minimally in studies limited to the last few years. Historical views of key variables may enable us to learn about processes of growth, cycles, and interactions that are now unknown. In addition, when properly analyzed, data from the past can be aggregated to yield reconstruction of global patterns in the past. At present, we have some idea of global patterns for today, but the past to which we compare it consists of records only from a collection of localities, and probably unrepresentative localities at that. Being able to compare the global patterns of today with global patterns in the past may provide us with a different idea of global social change.

Creating a global historical data resource, while a complex task, is also one that has become feasible. The organization of Big Data in history can now be accomplished, not only because of advances in information technology, but because of breakthroughs in communication and collaboration among historians and social scientists. The exciting advances of Big Data in the natural sciences provide encouragement and specific techniques that will draw historical data together. In the study of climate, a huge collaborative effort at an international level has developed models and empirical evidence on global climate in recent centuries and also in the distant past. In astronomy, there has been a parallel collection of great quantities of new data that give a steadily improving picture of the universe and its patterns of change – from the local level of our planetary system to the scale of the entire universe. In biology, a great research effort has just achieved a new level of precision in description and analysis of the human genome. The problems of creating a dataset on human history will be different from those in natural science fields, but the general level of feasibility of the project is roughly parallel.

This volume introduces the Collaborative for Historical Information and Analysis (CHIA, www.chia.pitt.edu) and its project for a world-historical archive. With a growing number of colleagues, I have been working since 2007 to build the project for a world-historical archive addressing variables in social sciences, health, and climate to document the past 400 years. The CHIA collaborative, based at the University of Pittsburgh, includes participants at universities in the U.S. and Europe – and at research centers in Africa, Latin America, and Asia. CHIA has now gained substantial initial

DOI: 10.1057/9781137378972

funding from the U.S. National Science Foundation (NSF), and smaller amounts of funding from several other sources. Concisely put, the purpose of CHIA is to create a single, comprehensive archive linking an immense range of historical data across space, time, topic, and scale. Fortunately, modern information technology will make it possible to achieve this objective through a virtual archive distributed across many sites (though it is necessary to have shared protocols and standards throughout). Historical data are huge in quantity and are deeply diverse in quality – but are the only source of information on change over time.

This book is to show how the task is being taken on. First, the book is to articulate, for scholars and policymakers, the need for a world-historical archive. Second, it is to attract collaborators to the project – developers of archive structure, contributors of data, and users and evaluators of the data resource. The third purpose of the book is to launch a broad and critical discussion on the ends and the means of a world-historical archive, especially by potential users of the archive, to clarify which paths of development will be most broadly useful. Fourth, the book is to compare the CHIA project with other large-scale data collection projects in social sciences and natural sciences, to obtain insights into the pitfalls and achievements of such projects and thereby help set priorities for CHIA.

This book is a comprehensive introduction to CHIA and its tasks. It is relatively technical, in that it attempts to describe most of the main tasks of CHIA and its archive, and to show how they connect to each other. Thus the book must address many fields of social sciences, natural sciences, humanities, and information science, and address their specialized vocabularies in doing so. Quite a different sort of introduction to CHIA focuses on the historical and social lessons that will result from the CHIA archive. It gives more details on why it is necessary to gather data about the history of the world as a whole, recent global changes, and how ordinary people will benefit from supporting and using the CHIA program. That introduction, available on the CHIA website, explains why every society should become involved in supporting the collection of historical data and study the results of this new historical resource (Manning 2013).

The first two chapters of this book convey the character of a global historical data resource and the social needs that will be met by such a resource. This initial chapter provides a tour through the facets of the CHIA project – its purpose, main areas of activity, the groups of people it

DOI: 10.1057/9781137378972

seeks to engage, and the challenges that it is likely to encounter. Chapter 2 begins with a fuller discussion of the need for big, global data in history, and follows up by describing the character and patterns of global historical data along with the nature and feasibility of the project.

Chapter 3 helps demonstrate the ability to collaborate, even in social sciences and history, on such a large project. It describes the specific objectives of CHIA and the way in which the project's collaborative structure is designed to bring broad geographic scope, great flexibility, local autonomy, and still benefit from strong organization and clear direction. The specific techniques for facilitating collaborative work are presented as innovations that have served CHIA well in its early stages and may prove more generally valuable. The chapter concludes with an explicit invitation to those who might become fellow workers on the archive, contributors of data, or users and evaluators of the data resource.

## Three missions in creating a world-historical data resource

Chapters 4, 5, and 6 address the specific missions of the overall project. The chapters introduce the interacting elements of 'the Archive', as illustrated in Figure 1.1. The Archive, also identified as the 'world-historical data resource', refers to the whole system of repository, documentation, and analysis. At the same time, each of the five levels within it is also seen as an archive. The Archive is a comprehensive, distributed, and linked repository and analytical system containing relational datasets. Datasets are maintained at distinct but overlapping levels of the Archive, from datasets newly received and beginning the process of incorporation to global, interdisciplinary collections of data along with the results of analysis and visualization. If we think of the Archive as a repository, we can say that it refers to all the files of data and applications that are accessible to the CHIA project, which may be held in a wide range of repositories. In terms of particular servers, they include a server in the School of Information Science at the University of Pittsburgh, the resources of the Pittsburgh Supercomputer Center, housed on the Cloud, and the CHIA files held within the Dataverse Network of Harvard University, which in turn are stored on the Cloud.

Figure 1.1 displays the Archive as a whole and many of the functions and processes within it. It shows the five principal levels of the overall

DOI: 10.1057/9781137378972

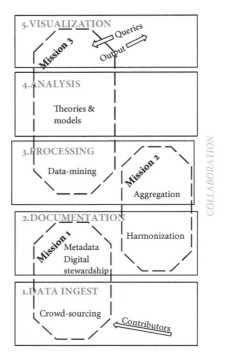

**FIGURE 1.1**    *World-historical data resource, showing functions and activities*

data resource and the three missions that link the levels by moving and transforming datasets from one level to the next. Each level consists of a distributed archive holding datasets that undergo a specific sort of housing and treatment – and each level is complicated by interactions and feedback loops. Here is a concise summary of the levels, followed by a fuller description of each. At Level 1, files contributed to CHIA are reviewed and archived in their original form for at least three distinctive purposes.[2] Files entered through the CHIA crowdsourcing ingest process and documented through the Col*Fusion application move into the Level 2 archive and by stages to the higher levels of CHIA. Level 3 holds files fully documented, harmonized and linkable to other CHIA files. Level 4 holds aggregated files created by the merging of existing CHIA files, up to the global level. Level 5 holds files including those created by analysis and visualization of the data. To keep track of the full range of files in the Archive, a system of administration and protocols is expanding progressively. Visitors and users of CHIA will be able to explore the

DOI: 10.1057/9781137378972

data at all five levels using the CHIA visualization tools, with simpler tools for Levels 1 and 2 and more elaborate ones for Levels 3, 4, and 5.

The Level 1 archive includes all the activities of CHIA crowdsourcing ingest and pre-processing. Its first element is the Data Hoover, a program designed to locate and 'hoover' (or 'vacuum') valuable historical datasets into the Archive. Second, contributors submit data through a crowd-sourcing process, in interaction with CHIA staff. Third, each incoming dataset undergoes a review to determine its character and its place or direction in the system is recommended. Fourth, each incoming dataset is archived, registered, and made available to CHIA users online, according to the specifications of Digital Stewardship. Fifth, those files that are to be incorporated into larger analysis may undergo Pre-processing. Sixth, there are two directions for additional analysis. First of these is the 'Spatio-Temporal Bridge', which focuses on spatial and temporal metadata. Its analysis reveals the spatio-temporal emphasis of numerous files in a given topical area. The advantage of this application is that, with minimal processing, it provides detailed information on the density of existing studies. Finally, datasets may be incorporated into the Col\*Fusion process for merging with the full set of files.

The Col\*Fusion process is the step that leads most clearly to the creation of a world-historical data resource because it is able to merge datasets through analysis and revision of their metadata. Col\*Fusion works through interaction of the contributor, the application itself, and with consultation by CHIA staff to upgrade and coordinate the description of data so that it is consistent with that of files already in the Level 2 archive. In this way a 'target schema', an overall system of metadata, develops steadily and maintains consistency as more data are incorporated into the Level 2 archive. The Col\*Fusion application has the additional advantage that it is able to merge the incoming file with existing files: through repetition, this process can lead to merger of multiple files.

Once in Level 2, each dataset undergoes 'harmonization', a set of processes that enables datasets to be linked more fully to other datasets. Details of harmonization include cleaning data of remaining errors, identifying overlaps and conflicts of datasets, establishment of consistent weights and measures, and confirming consistency among variables documented in different languages. As in Level 1, the datasets in Level 2 and higher levels of the Archive benefit from Digital Stewardship, the system of dataset preservation and citation. For these higher levels, citations of datasets refer not only to the original datasets submitted by contributors,

DOI: 10.1057/9781137378972

but also to the transformed datasets based upon submitted files. One key result of the ingest and harmonization of numerous datasets is the expansion of the overall 'target schema,' a consistent set of metadata on sources, time, space, topic, and transformations. The expanding system of metadata, facilitated by the work of CHIA staff, will contribute to the broader goal of approximating a world-historical ontology. Completion of this process of harmonization prepares datasets for transfer to Level 3 of the archive.

The advances of the CHIA project have implications going well beyond the project itself, especially in facilitating the merging of datasets. Since all of the work of CHIA is to be open-source and open-access, the combined processes of Col*Fusion and harmonization can be used independently by researchers – outside of CHIA, if they wish. Using these techniques, researchers will be able to merge datasets selected for their own purposes. While the Col*Fusion process – verifying the documentation of each variable and resolving inconsistencies in data definition – involves some labor, it addresses a problem in data analysis that has long been resistant to resolution. That is, the thousands of social science datasets archived in major repositories have tended to remain isolated from one another. That is, while datasets can be connected through analysis of the file-level metadata on their sources and overall characteristics, there has not previously been an application that connects the variable-level metadata within datasets. The combined process of Col*Fusion and harmonization, though it is still in development, seems destined to permit the full merger of independent datasets and, through recurring application of the process, widespread aggregation of datasets.

The processes in Level 3 of the Archive focus first on aggregation and then on data-mining. Aggregation, conducted by CHIA staff, is the continued merger of datasets to the point where they provide observations on macro-regional and global dynamics of the variables. Aggregation of datasets moves along at least three axes: expanding the geographic scope of datasets, expanding temporal scope, and expanding topical scope – the range of topical variables included in each dataset. The aggregated datasets include extended metadata, to document the steps in aggregation along with all previous metadata. All of the datasets, from local to global and over various time frames, are then ready to be advanced to Level 4 of the archive. Before that transfer, however, CHIA conducts an exercise in data-mining within the Level 3 archive. That is, using numeric techniques of analysis and high-speed computation, the datasets in the Level

DOI: 10.1057/9781137378972

3 archive are explored to seek out relationships among variables that have not previously been suspected. The results of data-mining are expected to be useful in expanding the types of analysis conducted in Level 4.

Level 4 of the data resource is that of formal analysis relying on the theories of social science and natural science. In the context of this world-historical data resource, theories may be extended beyond their normal domains and encounter each other. That is, the work in Level 4 is expected to yield new empirical results on relationships in global history, and it is also expected to lead to expansion in the scope of social science theory. The other principal task in Level 4 is that of combining data and theory to estimate missing values in historical data, especially for those early times and large areas of the world where data are scarce. As with other data, the simulated data are to be documented thoroughly. Of course there are certain problems of circularity with using theory-based algorithms to estimate missing data and then using the missing data to verify theory-based hypotheses, but there are also techniques for minimizing circularity. The results of analysis and simulation will yield new data and datasets: these datasets, along with those imported to Level 4, are then moved to Level 5.

The fifth and final level is that of visualization – that is, display of the results of queries and analysis by users. Visualization may provide responses to questions from the most basic to the most complex. For instance, it may provide straightforward observations of historical data, such as quantities of silver in circulation, quantities of rice output, or sizes of populations. But it may also include the interactions among these three factors with each other and with other factors. Visualization may take various forms, focusing on spatial representation, statistical analysis, graphical representation, or representation of multi-dimensional models. The users of visualization techniques to explore the CHIA Archive will include CHIA staff, seeking to evaluate their work on lower levels, researchers analyzing world-historical patterns, and a general audience including teachers and students, which may pose queries ranging from the basic to the advanced. While substantial research remains to be completed on this section of the CHIA Archive, that research will consider the range of advances in techniques of visualization that have emerged recently in the social sciences and especially in the natural sciences. Insofar as possible, the results of such visualization are retained and included within the system, so that the Level 5 archive is the most complete throughout the system.

DOI: 10.1057/9781137378972

At present and for the foreseeable future, the work of *building* the CHIA Archive includes three types of work: infrastructure, data incorporation, and modeling. The advance of these three types of work will make CHIA into a substantial archive that will sustain intensive analysis and visualization. (The work of *applying* the CHIA Archive, through analysis and visualization, takes place at every stage and should continue over a long time.) In practice, much of the text in Chapters 4, 5, and 6 is devoted to infrastructure: describing the specific tasks being carried out to construct the overall data resource. The most substantial funding that CHIA has received so far is for that purpose: the creation of an infrastructure – in information technology and in administrative organization – that will enable the ingest and analysis of unprecedented quantities of historical data. The U.S. National Science Foundation's 'Building Community and Capacity' initiative is intended 'to enable research communities to develop visions, teams, and capabilities dedicated to creating new, large-scale, next-generation data resources and relevant analytic techniques to advance fundamental research for the SBE and EHR sciences. Successful proposals will outline activities that will have significant impacts across multiple fields by enabling new types of data-intensive research'.[3] The award to CHIA, totaling US$ 600,000, is not an immense grant in comparison to the funding of fully operating research projects, but it provides a substantial opportunity for CHIA to become ready, in three years, to incorporate the many historical datasets for which it is designed.

While the text of Chapters 4, 5, and 6 focuses on the building of infrastructure, the organizational structure of those same chapters highlights the collection and processing of data. Processing of historical data is the main work that will take place once the infrastructure is in place. This work is described in terms of three CHIA missions, and each mission is to move the data from one stage in the CHIA process to the next: Mission 1 is to assemble and document the data; Mission 2 is to harmonize and aggregate the data; Mission 3 is to analyze and visualize the data. The tasks are distributed widely among the groups participating in CHIA, and are supported by a range of types of funding.

## Big Data comparisons across time and disciplines

Chapters 7 and 8 demonstrate lessons from previous projects in social sciences and parallel constructions of Big Data in other fields. The

DOI: 10.1057/9781137378972

discussion addresses pitfalls and achievements in these projects, summing up their lessons by restating the priorities recommended for CHIA. Chapter 7 narrates the evolution of large-scale research in three broad areas: social sciences, climatology, and genomics. It may at first appear that the extraordinary success of the modeling of climate and the analysis of genomes for humans and other species exceeds the accomplishments of the social sciences by so far that nothing is gained by their comparison. The points of departure differed greatly: in social science it was the effort to generate national statistics, in climatology it was the attempt to predict weather, and in genomics it was the desire to understand how proteins and cells reproduced. But as I seek to show, the range of dynamics in each of these fields of research shows that much is shared. Once each group began to expand its scale of analyzing and modeling its subject at a planetary scale, and once theory and empirical data (both contemporary and historical) developed interactively, the parallels among these distinct fields became truly instructive. In particular, analysis of human society can gain much by studying the collaborative and interactive work that has taken place in climatology, genomics, and other fields of natural science. Many lessons can be drawn from climatic and genetic modeling in order to facilitate data collection, modeling, and analysis for human society over time.

In climate, the key issue has been analysis of temperature and precipitation, as these have changed with time. Continued exploration of those issues led to encountering other important issues and to a comprehensive analysis of climate. Studies of genomics began with the mechanism of genetic change, but the accumulation of knowledge suddenly shifted emphasis into study of the history and evolution of humans and of many other species. For human society, the initial issues of concern are more numerous and more complex. To simplify them, we focus on population, human–natural interaction, development, governance, and socioeconomic inequality. Still, connection and modeling of these interacting issues, requiring complex collaboration among researchers, leads in directions analogous to those of climate modeling.

Chapter 8 concludes the book with a statement of current CHIA priorities and the processes by which those priorities will be modified over time. With the CHIA approach, once we can report summary evidence on key variables worldwide, we will know where the evidence came from and what degree of uncertainty they entail.[4] That will be a sharp contrast to currently available global statistics, in either print or electronic

DOI: 10.1057/9781137378972

form, which give no uncertainty levels and generally do not specify the source(s). The CHIA plan is to focus on collecting data for the era prior to 1950. We recognize that, for years since 1950, much progress has been achieved in developing global data through the energies of modern national governments, the United Nations, the World Bank and other groups. The work of CHIA will focus initially on earlier times, for which data are less well-developed yet equally important. The project is to focus especially on the data that have yet to be digitized, yet to be published, and on the regions where even handwritten documents are scarce. As the collection of pre-1950 historical data becomes larger and better organized, CHIA's attention will turn to linking pre-1950 global data with data on the world since 1950.

The chapters to follow expand on each of the points above. On one hand, this little book will emphasize the range of challenges to resolve and obstacles to surmount before we can create a world-historical data resource. On the other hand the same work is intended to demonstrate that comprehensive and energetic collaboration can solve those problems. Within just a few years, we can achieve a strong beginning for global historical analysis in the social sciences. In the same process, we can document past links between human society and natural processes. The biggest and most important result of this collaborative project will be the creation of a worldwide historical data resource on human society. The formulation of world-historical data will facilitate the needed research on social patterns at levels from the local to the global.

The CHIA project pledges to maintain open-source, open-access, non-proprietary standards throughout its work in constructing a world-historical archive. As we see it, the contributions of this project belong to everybody. Further, CHIA pledges to maintain high standards of attribution: the contributors of data must be recognized for their submissions and system developers must also be recognized for their contributions. Two types of problems, however, will arise at every stage in this work. First, CHIA faces problems of collaboration – the social organization of this collective work. The work requires tight overall organization, but also requires a maximum of flexibility and independence for participants at every level. To succeed, it must become a very large-scale project with links to every corner of the world. Second, CHIA must address problems of capacity – of sufficiently high-level technology and of sufficiently large resources in space and funding to carry out the many demands of the project. Mission 1, gathering data, focuses on *collaboration* in

DOI: 10.1057/9781137378972

the collection and sharing of historical data. It emphasizes building *new capacity* with its focus on peer review of datasets and by using a crowdsourcing application that enables contributors to submit data easily from remote locations. Mission 2, aggregating data, focuses on *collaboration* in collecting data from all areas of the world. It focuses on *new capacity* through the creation of a unified global archive, relying on harmonization of heterogeneous data and the aggregation and linking of data at all levels. Mission 3, visualizing and analyzing data, focuses on *collaboration* through incorporating data from parallel groups involved in assembling global data. It focuses on *new capacity* through developing multi-dimensional systems for representing data and through application of data-mining techniques to locate unsuspected linkages within the global dataset.

For scholars in many fields who are being invited to join in the work of constructing the world-historical archive, this book is intended to convey the range of tasks, the types of theory and experience necessary, and the sorts of collaboration – both local and worldwide – that it will take to create this archive and then to begin analyzing social change with it. This short book is therefore complex and multi-faceted, in reflection of the complex world we live in. The purpose is to make the case that today's social scientists can handle the complexity – that we have the capability to create a global picture of our society in past and present, and therefore have more conscious influence over our future.

# Notes

1   Among the most extensive and valuable national archives are the British Archives at Kew, near London; the imperial Chinese archives in Beijing, and the Turkish national archives in Istanbul. Other major national archives are those of Portugal, Spain, the Netherlands, Russia, and Japan.

2   As of this writing, the CHIA Level 1 Archive is open to submission of datasets by contributors; selected datasets, through documentation and merging, have entered the Level 2 Archive. Public users may conduct analysis and visualization of these files through the CHIA portal (CHIA).

3   'SBE' refers to social, behavioral, and economic sciences; 'EHR' refers to education and human resources.

4   This goal requires that, insofar as possible, metadata and uncertainly levels be documented at the level of individual observations and not simply as file-level aggregates.

DOI: 10.1057/9781137378972

# 2
# The Need to Know our Global Past

**Abstract:** *Dramatic changes of the present suggest to some that we need not worry about the past. But these same changes have revealed important new knowledge about the past and have convinced leading researchers that we are still governed by past processes. Continental drift, genetic change, and social history each show our tight connection to the past. This chapter identifies key historical variables and shows how they reveal change and continuity over the past five centuries. It emphasizes that, to document the history of human society, one needs to account for numerous factors interacting in a social system at local and global scales. Nevertheless, new technology makes it possible to create a large-scale connected record of the human experience.*

Keywords: historical variables; social system

Manning, Patrick. *Big Data in History*. Basingstoke: Palgrave Macmillan, 2013. DOI: 10.1057/9781137378972.

DOI: 10.1057/9781137378972

All of us are making plans for a global future. Leaders in government, the economy, in society – along with ordinary people at every level – are trying to keep global change in mind as they make plans. The periodic global summits on environmental issues provide a large-scale example: they met in Stockholm (1972), Rio (1992), Kyoto (1997), Johannesburg (2002), Copenhagen (2009), and Rio (2012). The World Bank seeks to develop projections of global economic change, especially in response to worldwide 'Millennium Goals' adopted by the United Nations in 2000. Military leaders in the U.S., the NATO alliance, China, Russia, Japan, and other countries make contingency plans for global conflict. We also see plans and projections on global health, energy use, and levels of education. Families and individuals conduct planning for a global future by identifying career choices, education plans, allocations of family wealth, and even marriage choices.

But in proposing plans for the global future, what information do the planners have about the global past? What hints do the planners have about the actual specifics of global conditions, even the conditions of today? What errors might result from assuming that the patterns of a certain city or country will be an adequate proxy for past global realities? Are the current changes in cultural fashion or in unfolding social movements really 'for the first time', as the participants commonly claim? In sum, it is risky to make decisions at the global level while remaining blind to past patterns. One cannot conduct global analysis without global data. Despite the intensive development of national-level data, we have little detail on global patterns in population, social and political organization, economic flows, and how these relate to health and climate. We know that governance, in the present, is a crisis-laden issue worldwide. For the past, however, we have well-organized information only on the governance of European empires and nations, not on the many other communities that were ancestral to so much of humanity today.

The continued and widespread willingness to ignore the need for global-historical data means, implicitly, either that one assumes that the past doesn't matter in setting policy for the future or that global questions can be answered by scattered, local data. It would be best to test both of those assumptions against historical data. Fortunately, resources are available to conduct such a test. We now have the capability to document comprehensively the global patterns of *today* and to compare them with global patterns of *the past*. For the past, the CHIA project is to create

DOI: 10.1057/9781137378972

data at the world-historical level: global totals and their changes, broken down by space, time, and topic.

To develop dependable global-historical data we must overcome a range of obstacles – organizational, technical, and theoretical, plus the obstacle of misconceptualizing history. Responses to the first three types of obstacles provide the subject matter for Chapters 3, 4, 5, and 6. Organizational obstacles include the problems of facilitating large-scale collaboration among researchers in many fields, and the differences in data collection separating wealthy and poor regions of the world or separating sparsely documented and densely documented domains. Technical obstacles include the heterogeneity of the data; the complexities of data description; the amount of skilled labor required to digitize documents in print, manuscript, or image form; and the problems of automating the ingest, documentation, and aggregation of data up to the global level. Theoretical obstacles include the 'silos' of various disciplines (in which researchers speak only to others of the same discipline). Thus, micro and macro theories within given disciplines are disconnected, disciplines connect only marginally to each other, and global study is neglected.

The present chapter addresses the obstacles brought by weak conceptualization of history. Too often, history is presented simply as celebratory narrative of distant ancestors, with little attention to the logic of historical change or to the multiple scales at which the historical past has unfolded. Social scientists commonly treat history as 'background' – as information on past times that may be parallel to their current study, but remains excluded from the actual analysis. Further, and not only in the minds of school children, events and processes of the past may be explained solely in terms of the individual agency of leading figures rather than in terms of social structures and dynamics. Even when social forces are admitted to historical interpretation, history is often presented as if its driving dynamics acted only on kingdoms and nations, so that individual lives on one side and global patterns on another side were determined fully by the policymakers at national levels. (If many people maintained such oversimplified pictures of the past, no wonder that they found globalization – the unmistakable presence of global patterns in economics and culture from the 1990s – to be unprecedented.)

Such weaknesses in conceptualization of history are compounded by weaknesses in conceptualization of the world, either in present or past times. Some visions of 'the world' leave out whole continents, notably

DOI: 10.1057/9781137378972

Africa and South America, despite their immense populations. Or there exist assumptions that many parts of the world survived in total isolation until they were opened up recently to global contact. Too often the world is modeled as if human society centers on one or two metropolitan cores, the unique sources of innovation and culture. Such models leave most regions as passive peripheries, which can only act through acceptance or rejection of innovations from the center.

As an example of how large-scale historical analysis can fall short of being global, let us take the study of empires. Empires from Rome and Han China to the British Empire have erected imposing political and cultural structures. They have surely played a role in world history, interacting with other empires and with peoples beyond imperial frontiers. In historical studies, however, empires are mostly investigated one at a time, with a focus on their rise and fall and on their principal wars. They are studied occasionally as they interact with a competitor (Spain vs. France or Russia vs. the Ottomans) but almost never as interactive parts of a worldwide political system. Thus the British Empire, even at its most dominant, held only a portion of the world's imperial possessions: actions of other empires constrained the British. It should also be possible to study the world as a social and political system and to investigate the role of empires within that system.

The field of world history has developed forcefully and effectively during the past two decades, and has clarified conceptual dimensions of global analysis over time. World historians have updated the stereotyped oversimplifications of global patterns and have released from isolation the narratives of localities and societies. In place of stereotyped and fragmented histories, world historians are developing analyses of interactions among regions and among the many arenas of human life. World history shows the existence of long-term trends, continuities, and cycles in human experience, revealing that rates of change in different areas of experience (e.g., family and economy) are not the same. World historians are now making advances in documenting the interplay among scales (Benton 2008). Still, the impressive advances in world-historical documentation and analysis went on for some time without a campaign to create world-historical data. Further, in the frustrating feedback loop with which we began, global patterns in social science have not been explored in much detail for lack of global data. Such world-historical data can only be created through a large-scale project – a collaborative successor to the many past projects that created national historical data.

DOI: 10.1057/9781137378972

Fascinating and groundbreaking analyses await us once we assemble historical data systematically at regional and global levels. We will be able to trace the rise and fluctuation of global systems of money and credit (Reinhart and Rogoff 2009). We will have detail on shifting global patterns of population, mortality, and migration. We will trace the unfolding of governance at local, national, and imperial levels, and changing systems of family structure.

## Types of historical data and historical patterns

Figure 2.1 displays an interpretation of types of historical data. This is a limited selection of variables, intended to be illustrative rather than definitive. Any reader will be able to pick out additional issues in history that would be worthy of documentation as part of a world-historical data resource. But the assumption of CHIA, as illustrated in Figure 2.1, is that a partial selection of an overlapping range of variables can provide the basis for a useful, initial investigation of global-historical patterns. Figure 2.1 begins with population, on the assumption that the human population is the most basic element of human society, and that the records on population size by age, sex, and rates of birth, death, and migration are factors of primary interest. Three more groupings of variables have the advantage of being relatively available and highly relevant to major social concerns: these are data on development, governance, and the interactions of human society and the natural world, especially through climate and health. Still other issues, while of great significance for our understanding of society at levels from the local to the global, are more difficult to document; thus, it is more difficult to locate data on volumes of production than to find prices of the goods produced.

All of the variables indicated in Figure 2.1 can be assessed at micro and macro levels, and at levels in between. Within each category (for instance, labor) there are many more variables that could be defined and documented. That is, labor includes household, agricultural, artisanal, industrial, and bureaucratic labor, with varying roles by age, sex, and status (such as free vs. slave or bound): for a world-historical dataset, one must identify a simplified and yet appropriate selection of these for documentation (GCHLR).

Identifying and collecting historical data is one set of tasks, locating the patterns and processes linking historical evidence into narratives,

DOI: 10.1057/9781137378972

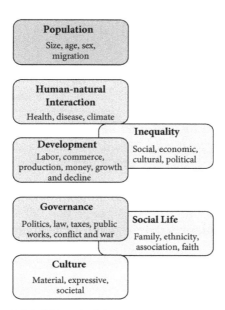

FIGURE 2.1   *Types of global-historical data*

dynamics, and analyses is quite another. In effect, to get from historical narrative to analysis of patterns, we *model* the variations in historical factors by simplifying them. One can model spatial dynamics in terms of diffusion, crystallization, or links in networks. One can model temporal dynamics in terms of episodes, crises, growth, decline, and cycles. One can model topical interactions in terms of innovation, response, and macro-cultural choices. One can model interactions in scale through hierarchy, networks, and inequality. To provide some examples of modeling strategies: one can identify cycles of inequality in history; cycles of gender relations; cultural choice among societies holding large vs. small numbers of persons in slavery; and the contrasts among hierarchy in political control from elite levels, 'history from below' as subaltern groups influence overall social relations, and networks connecting collaborators in various social groups.

The next section applies this general selection of historical data, as shown in Figure 2.1, to a concise review of the past five centuries of world history, to indicate that the analysis of a dataset and a narrative of historical change can be seen as parallel ways of representing the same underlying processes. It is expected that a combination of narrative and analysis will elicit additional information about the past.

DOI: 10.1057/9781137378972

# Global history seen through a big-data resource

Let us imagine that we already had global data on human society. Imagine that we had data on numerous historical variables throughout the world, reflecting global parallels and interaction. Then one could imagine a history constructed out of a large dataset. What follows is a compressed narrative of the past five centuries of human history, relying especially on a few variables, as if they were drawn from a dataset. The central factors in this concise global story are human experiences with *lifespan, migration, textiles, silver, empires, social inequality*, and *epidemic*. Each of these variables has been selected from the more general categories displayed in Figure 2.1: lifespan and migration fall within the category of population; textiles and silver within development; empires within governance; social inequality within inequality; and epidemics within human–natural interactions. Even this simplified view of world history shows the differences in local and global patterns. It shows surprising variations and interactions and raises questions about global change.

Let us begin with population and lifespan: five centuries ago, world population was slightly more than half a billion, not even one-tenth of what it is today. World regions in rank order of population were China, India, Africa, Europe, the Americas, and other parts of Asia (Southeast, West, and Central). Interestingly, the regional rankings of population were very similar to those of today. At that time, lifespans averaged some 30 years, slightly lower in tropical areas. All regions experienced high levels of infant mortality, accompanied by high levels of mortality of mothers in childbirth.

Expanding oceanic voyages brought migration of sailors, soldiers, and merchants. Global trade required an effective currency: candidates were African gold, Chinese copper, and even pearls or diamonds. But the opening in 1550 of great mines in Bolivia and Mexico ensured that silver would become the world's main currency. Each year, Spanish fleets carried silver to Seville and single galleons carried silver across the Pacific to Manila. Buyers in Amsterdam, Moscow, Constantinople, Bombay, and Canton competed for a share of Mexican silver. In exchange, Chinese silks, Indian cottons, European woolens, and elegant ceramics traveled in opposite directions. But growing interregional contact brought serious problems as well. Sailors on long voyages suffered from scurvy – a vitamin C deficiency from lack of vegetables. Human contact also led to the spread of infectious disease. In the Americas, higher death rates

DOI: 10.1057/9781137378972

brought disastrous population decline during the sixteenth century as epidemics of Old World diseases arose in communities that had never before experienced them. Similarly, smallpox spread in Africa and syphilis reached not only Europe but Japan.

Expanded social interactions of several types accompanied global travel and trade. Great empires arose suddenly in about 1500 in India and Iran, and also for the Ottomans, Spanish, Portuguese, and Russians – then the Songhai empire in West Africa fell. In about 1650 another set of empires arose, partly displacing the previous powers: the Dutch, French, English, and the Qing state in China. Settlers from Europe, Africa, and Asia moved to crowded lands and to empty spaces. European migrants to Asia and the Americas, mostly in military service, were outnumbered by African migrants to the Americas and the Mediterranean, mostly in slavery. In the eighteenth century, the now-underpopulated Americas' population growth began with the arrival of European and African migrants; in western Africa, population began to decline because of enslavement. Indian cottons went to Africa in exchange for many of these captives. Still, silver flowed from Bolivia and Mexico.

The Atlantic, Indian, and Pacific oceans became increasingly linked due to commerce and migration, and eighteenth-century health conditions gradually improved in Eurasia and the Americas. Atlantic empires came to depend on forced labor to produce sugar, tobacco, coffee; Asian empires produced sugar and opium. The English and French fought a century of wars on every continent. The English displaced the Mughals in India, but lost the United States. The empires of England, France, Spain, and Portugal declined in size from 1780 to 1820 – only China and Russia maintained their size. Silver mining declined in independent Bolivia but expanded in Mexico. Now it was merchants from the independent United States who shipped silver to Europe, Asia, and Africa. England, relying on slave-grown American cotton fiber, began to displace India as the main global source of cotton textiles. Emancipation of slaves in the Americas and of serfs in Eastern Europe and Russia brought migration of newly freed people. The rise of steamships overlapped with emancipation.

From 1850, steamships changed commercial transport and revolutionized migration. Migrants first left Europe – Irish in the lead. Overall, this great wave of migration from 1850 to 1940 evened out world population. Migrants went mostly from densely populated regions – Europe, India, China, and Russia – to take up work in regions with sparser

DOI: 10.1057/9781137378972

population. Over 30 million each went to the Americas, Southeast Asia, and Northeast Asia. Africans too continued to migrate, now from one part of the continent to another. Emancipation and migration worldwide brought new social mixtures that generated new ideas of racial hierarchy on every continent. With the rapidity of migration, cholera now spread from India to many world regions; with the expansion of mining, an epidemic of tuberculosis spread around the world. At the same time, new industrial economies became rich by comparison to the previously leading economies of China and India. Shortages of money in an expanding global economy pushed up the value of silver and gold. Gold rushes broke out from 1848 to the end of the century, when South African deep mines were established. But still the Mexican silver continued to flow from the mines. Britain led in creating a gold standard for international money from 1850 through 1930, though silver remained the main monetary metal.

New social problems and huge gaps of inequality developed during the nineteenth century. As the steamships carried migrants and commodities rapidly and on schedule among all ports of the world, they also carried microbes. Cholera, which had previously been restricted to India, now showed up in ports throughout the world. Typhoid, tuberculosis, and other bacterial diseases spread rapidly around the world. Levels of health, education, and income improved dramatically in Europe, North America, and Japan, but also with growing gaps between the rich and poor. China and India became economically poor regions during the century. Remarkably, lifespans grew in many areas of the world during the nineteenth century, though not in Africa, where expanded enslavement reduced lifespans. Still, terrible droughts and horrible famines broke out in climate shifts that are now understood as the El Niño Southern Oscillation. The results brought great loss of life in the 1870s and 1880s in India, China, Brazil, and Africa. The single greatest epidemic was that of influenza in 1918: wartime and commercial ties spread a virus that killed many more people than those who died in the war.

Empires expanded again, if briefly. Late in the nineteenth century, European powers absorbed all of Africa and the Pacific, and most of Asia. Yet they collided in two world wars, from 1914 to 1945, bringing revolution and ultimate collapse of all but two of the imperial powers. Imperial decline from 1945 – 'decolonization' – brought recognition of a hundred additional nations on all the continents and in the islands. The United Nations arose as a global forum and a Cold War pitted the U.S.

DOI: 10.1057/9781137378972

and the Soviet Union against each other until 1992. Money changed, as its supply depended primarily on the checking account balances available in the U.S. Even so, the ups and downs in silver trade, still coming mostly from Mexico, remained an important factor in the global economy. Textile manufacture moved back to Asia – especially Japan, India, and China. Yet synthetic fabrics – nylon, acrylic, polyester, and more – supplemented and displaced cotton and woolens. Epidemics of measles and polio grew in intensity until the creation of vaccines reduced mortality. Another long wave of migration began in the 1960s, but international migration was smaller than before in volume because of national and racial restrictions, and migrants were now treated as a threat rather than tolerated. More significantly, migration built huge cities on every continent, and made human population more uneven.

The world of the twenty-first century brought new inequalities and new equality. Labeling and hierarchical ranking of people by 'race', which crystallized in the seventeenth century and expanded in the nineteenth century, gradually declined. Higher education served wealthy countries and wealthy families, but the great global disparities in literacy and lifespan separating rich lands from poor lands declined. By 2010, the average lifespan worldwide exceeded 70 years. African countries remain behind in lifespan (especially those hit hard by the AIDS pandemic), yet African lifespans nearly doubled between 1950 and 2010. More than ever, however, economic inequality continued to expand within nations and between nations, separating poor from wealthy countries and poor families from rich families.

In this hurried but complicated narrative of global interaction, only a few key factors were used to recount human history. Adding in such factors as family and environmental change would add to the complexity and the connections. The story of each factor depends on change in the others. Documenting the global interactions in human society is a substantial task, and it may lead to results that are surprising. A world-historical data resource – Big Data on the human past – will give us a better version of large and small contours in the overall story.

The resulting interpretation is not a straightforward tale of progress, but a set of overlapping stories. Human society is too complex and multi-variate to be simplified into a single tale. Here, an attempt has been made to recount a brief global narrative based on an imagined global dataset. It does show some overall patterns and some unexpected connections. Table 2.1 provides a hint on the techniques for developing a

DOI: 10.1057/9781137378972

TABLE 2.1    *Some global changes and linkages, 1500–2000*

| Change in historical variables | Interaction of historical variables |
| --- | --- |
| ▶ Population growth and redistribution, fluctuating migration | ▶ Empires facilitated migration |
| ▶ Successive centers of textile production | ▶ Technology & politics in textiles |
| ▶ Silver: economies grew faster than silver supply | ▶ Competition of silver, gold, paper money |
| ▶ Empires expanded, warred, and declined | ▶ Imperial heritage in language and culture |
| ▶ Social inequality grew with development | ▶ Social movements demanded equality |
| ▶ New diseases arose as society changed | ▶ Immunity improved with nutrition |

global analysis out of the preceding narrative. On the left, the table lists patterns of change in individual variables; on the right it includes the same individual variables in bivariate or multi-variate changes. Let us begin with the univariate analysis of a single factor, such as the quantity of silver coin in circulation: one can trace silver quantities at all scales from local to global, the variation in silver quantities across space, the dynamics of changing silver quantities over time, and the interactions linking silver quantities by scale, region, and time.

More generally, for a global analysis of historical change, one must consider a whole range of univariate and multi-variate changes. This analysis can begin with global totals and averages in population, textiles, silver, imperial control, social conflict, disease (though it will also take account of data on these variables from the local up to the global scale). Then the analysis can explore types of temporal dynamics (episodes, cycles, growth), spatial dynamics (from diffusion to crystallization of innovations over a wide area), and topical dynamics (such as shifts in textile fabrics and centers of output). Further still, the interpretation can extend to many other factors – on race, religion, sport, gender, education, or literature. The potentialities of high-speed computing will make it possible to consider many of these factors at once, and to discover important relationships in human social change that are now not known. Studies in world history have already advanced sufficiently to affirm that there exists a history at the global level that identifies the most outstanding patterns of global change, while also showing that patterns at individual and family levels can diverge from those at the continental level.[1] I hope

DOI: 10.1057/9781137378972

that this quick look at global-level change and interaction is enough to suggest that it is indeed important for us to learn more about the past patterns in human society, in order to anticipate which past patterns will continue and which will shift. Later sections of this book will provide further details on this concise discussion of the many types of analysis that can be conducted with a world-historical data resource.[2]

## The realistic potential for documenting the global past

Is it realistic to plan on creating a world-historical data resource? Recent technological advance, especially in electronic communication, certainly makes it easier. Electronic scanning can translate texts and images from analog to digital media: Google Books has pressed far ahead in digitizing existing print works. Creating a scan of an existing document preserves it in a new format, but we still need improved technology in scanning print and manuscript files so that they can automatically be translated into searchable, digital text.[3] The internet, which is gradually converging with telephone communication, makes it possible to communicate by voice, image, text, or data files anywhere in the world, if the relevant devices are available. Geographic Information Systems, which had become a successful commercial system by the 1980s, allowed for a steady expansion in spatial definition of electronic files. Also from the 1980s, the emergence of supercomputing systems brought a steady emphasis on large-scale storage and analysis, working notably on climate. Computational systems involving the interaction of large numbers of variables and big datasets are an important part of this development. In a more recent development, the notion of collective intelligence (also known as 'crowdsourcing') has led to development of interfaces that enable large numbers of individuals to participate in collection and analysis of data on a given problem. In addition to these advances in technology, every discipline has expanded greatly the quantity and detail of its scientific knowledge. For instance, the great expansion in knowledge of the earth's climate history and the growing detail of history of disease are now ready to be combined with data on population and on agricultural production to give us clearer explanations of past changes and interactions of these variables.

But more than technology has changed. As argued here, we are beginning to develop an adequate conceptualization of the notion of global

DOI: 10.1057/9781137378972

patterns in human society. The idea of humanity as a whole has been understood for a long time, but primarily in the minds of a few visionaries: religious leaders envisioned the fate of all humanity in relation to the Creator; emperors considered the possibility of conquering the whole world; observers of the heavens compared the earth and its peoples to the heavenly bodies. Most humans spent their lives, however, focusing on their families, communities, and the states within which they lived – and they still do. In recent decades, nevertheless, almost everyone, for one reason or another, has come to spend time thinking about the world. This greater consciousness of the world and of human society is the first reason why it is now more possible than before to begin organizing information for the world as a whole.

Thinking globally means more than thinking about large areas. It means long periods of time and a wide range of topics. In addition, thinking globally means considering not just analysis at the largest scale, but the interactions of life all the way from the smallest scale to the largest and back again. An analogy with the field of biology is relevant. At one level, biology is the study of plants and animals – whole organisms. But plants and animals range from the tiny to the huge. In addition, biologists study the elements of each organism: they study cells and the constituents of cells, down to the molecular level.[4] At the other extreme, biologists study whole herds of one species, and they study great groups and evolutionary orders of plants and animals. Yet on every level it's all biology, and each part of the earth's great biological system interacts with many others. Similarly for human history: the view of the past, as we seek to document it, spans the full range from individual behavior to all of humanity, and it includes many types of activity over short and long periods of times. This sort of global understanding is now expanding in the social sciences.

Advances in conceptualization have not simply expanded in scale but have deepened in conceptualization. Within the past half century the notion of *systems* has developed productively in many areas of intellectual work. Systems are conceived as collections of interacting components that combine to sustain a larger whole. Systems are described in mechanical, thermodynamic, and organic terms, but also in social and environmental terms. Systems have structure, interconnectivity, and behavior. Some systems have purposes and exhibit adaptive behavior. Systems can be modeled in ways that distinguish closed from open systems; study of systems draws attention to information systems within

DOI: 10.1057/9781137378972

them. The application of systems-thinking is valuable at multiple levels in this project: we can treat an archive or an application as a system and we can treat the whole of historical society as a system. Linking these extremes, we can think of our participating colleagues – who build and maintain a world-historical data resource – as comprising a system in themselves.

Overall, I argue, the implementation of a global-historical data resource requires the unification of social science analysis. That is, the various social sciences, while they will continue to have their particular areas of application and specific purposes, must become more explicitly linked to each other. Important efforts have been made to trace links and commonalities in human social and historical behavior, but typically they have reached limits because they could only explain so much (Marx 1975, Compte 1967, Wallerstein 2001). More commonly, social scientists have been content to remain within their domains, explaining more and more about less and less. Social science analysts have sought out data of homogeneous quality and in finding it have tended to stay within national units, short time frames, and standardized data such as censuses. Crossing boundaries in time and space requires facing heterogeneity: it involves linking terms with changing meanings, linking maps with inconsistent scales, and addressing multiple languages, varying weights and measures. Policymakers are learning that long-term processes, previously ignored or undetected, have significant implications for the decisions they seek to implement: early events may have generated structures with lasting impact (Nunn 2009). In analysis, recent decades have seen dramatic change in the outlook and scholarly practice of social scientists and the techniques available to them. After the decline of colonialism and racialism, it has become easier for social scientists to seek out common experiences and motivations for our species as a whole rather than focus on uniqueness and socially specific attitudes defined by race or nation. Global and historical interests have grown among researchers in economic history, global politics, world systems, and global health (O'Brien 2006; Reinhart and Rogoff 2009; Gerring et al. 2005; Giddens 2003, Pomeranz 2000, Chase-Dunn and Babones 2006, Zimmer and Burke 2009; Bain et al. 2008).

In retrieval of social science data, the most obvious new technology is large-scale digitization of print, manuscript, and image data. For the organization of data, new techniques in GIS make it possible to define and analyze units that are modifiable in area and time (Southall 2011).

DOI: 10.1057/9781137378972

Other advances facilitate the exploration of problems of missing data: on one hand by getting useful information out of incomplete datasets; on the other hand by using advanced techniques of simulation and estimation to fill in the blanks (Honaker and King 2010, Manning 2010). Collaboration, meanwhile, has advanced more slowly in social sciences than in natural sciences. The inherited notion of the individual investigator is still valuable in every field: in astronomy, for instance, individual amateur astronomers still make important contributions to the field. But for historical studies, learning how to conduct collaborative research, write co-authored papers, and jointly seek support from major institutions is essential for large-scale analysis. While patient individual work has chipped into this barrier, the main hope for advancement lies in a large-scale campaign of data retrieval, transformation, and flexible integration that will make historical data accessible for global analysis.

## Notes

1    For instance, geologists' detailed identification of the timing, location, and force of volcanic eruptions over the past millennium has enabled historians to link these eruptions to episodes of cooling, famine, social upheaval, and political revolution. As a result, the logic of historical change is now seen within a more complex and interactive frame.

2    For other discussions of categories of historical interaction, see Chapters 6 and 8.

3    Even for years in which PDF files existed for data on U.S. disease surveillance, Project Tycho™ at Pitt had to re-enter all the data manually into digital files in order to create a searchable file. See Chapter 4 for further details.

4    For an engaging display of multiple and overlapping scales, see 'The Scale of the Universe 2', http://htwins.net.

DOI: 10.1057/9781137378972

# 3
# CHIA: Its Collaborative Mission, Structure, and Innovation

**Abstract:** *CHIA seeks to stimulate broad and active participation in the collaborative work of building a global historical data resource. To do so, CHIA must carry out the best practices in design, project administration, decentralization, project review, and innovation – and do so across disciplines, institutions, continents, and language groups. The balance of local autonomy with direction from headquarters is crucial: crowdsourcing calls on the general public to gather and document data; peer review of datasets requires commentary by independent-minded scholars; yet harmonizing and aggregating data requires a tightly organized project staff. For the director and Steering Committee, setting appropriate priorities is a balancing act of coordinating and sustaining CHIA's three complementary missions. Yet the enterprise can go ahead because of the widespread devotion to history.*

**Keywords:** coordinating; crowdsourcing; headquarters; local autonomy

Manning, Patrick. *Big Data in History*. Basingstoke: Palgrave Macmillan, 2013. DOI: 10.1057/9781137378972.

## Background and objectives of CHIA

Philosopher George Santayana understood the need for a large-scale historical resource long before it was feasible to create one. He warned (in 1901) that, 'Those who cannot remember the past are condemned to repeat it.' Less known, but likely as important, is his challenge that 'a man's feet should be planted in his country, but his eyes should survey the world'. The Collaborative for Historical Information and Analysis (CHIA) exists to accelerate and empower research surveying the global human record. As a public system, it will be used synergistically by policymakers making decisions, scholars identifying global processes, and educators developing student skills in global analysis. It will ingest comprehensive, multi-disciplinary data and provide tools to uncover the patterns of social interaction and the processes driving these interactions. Its research and analysis will integrate the approaches of social, health, and environmental sciences with those of information sciences. The result, an improved understanding of past patterns in society at all levels, is fundamental to assessing future challenges and predicting the success of proposed solutions.

CHIA is a collaboration of scholars in social sciences, information sciences, and natural sciences from institutions in the United States and several other parts of the world. It has been formed to respond to the need for world-historical data in the social sciences and in recognition of the current advances in the potential for assembling such data. CHIA took form in 2011 as a new initiative launched by veterans of several earlier campaigns to collect, preserve, archive, and analyze social science data on a large scale. In a step typical of the new type of academic work, the founding meeting took place by internet discussion rather than in a single room. The group adopted a comprehensive approach, seeking to emphasize new conceptions, not just accumulation of data. Aspects of the work as identified by CHIA include the data, a place to put data, keeping track of all the different types of data, documenting individual data (by time, place, topic, and scale), gaining a sense of the links among data as seen through theory, conducting advanced analysis to discover significant patterns within the data, and making the entire resource available to researchers, teachers, and students everywhere.

The long-term purpose of CHIA – in the time frame of perhaps a decade – is to facilitate the creation and maintenance of historical data sets from local to global levels, from short term to long term, linking

DOI: 10.1057/9781137378972

variables on many areas of human experience. The resultant summation of human experience can reveal the varying patterns and dynamics of social change. While past social, economic, and cultural dynamics may not carry automatically into the future, they should not be neglected in our attempts to make plans and form policy. The Collaborative intends to link social sciences to each other and to the principal problems in human society, at scales from the local to the global over the past four centuries and into the future. The Collaborative seeks to encourage a culture of data sharing among social scientists. And it expects to develop a global, integrative repository and analytical framework supporting specific research projects on four domains of social life: human–natural interaction, population change, development of socio-economic inequality, and governance (local and global). New knowledge of these past patterns will surely shape policy formulation.

The Collaborative evolved out of acquaintances at a range of academic meetings in fields including geographic information systems, social science and social science history meetings in the U.S. and Europe, digital humanities meetings, and initiatives such as the Global Economic History Network. The result was coalescence of scholars with similar or interlinked goals and skills, sharing an interest in large-scale data and analysis in social sciences, through visits and exchanges among research groups, development of internal university support for research, and then cross-university collaboration. Humphrey Southall, working from 1988 on Great Britain Historical GIS, developed immense analytical skill in electronic documentation of maps and in categorizing places over time. The Center for Geographic Analysis at Harvard, led by Peter Bol, conducted widespread consulting and also built China Historical GIS. The Institute for Quantitative Social Science, led by Gary King and Mercè Crosas, built on previous work to create an advanced data repository, the Dataverse Network. John Gerring and James Mahoney collected widespread data on colonialism, with NSF support, then transformed the study into a more general investigation of global political and social change. Ruth Mostern, with experience at the Electronic Cultural Atlas Initiative (ECAI) since 1997, created a GIS-based dataset on the politics of Song China. The International Institute of Social History in Amsterdam, a long-time supporter of archival work but also of social science analysis, developed a historical Labour Relations Collaborative as one of its numerous research projects. This project, beginning in 2008 with support from the Netherlands Organization for Scientific Research

DOI: 10.1057/9781137378972

(NWO) and the Gerda Henkel Stiftung, not only provided relevant data, but modeled effectively the best practices for building a coherent data collection out of the decentralized work of scholars in many countries.

At the University of Pittsburgh, as at Harvard and at IISH, collaboration spread through the institution. Two small grants in 2007 to Patrick Manning from the School of Arts and Sciences and Office of the Provost, plus energetic collaboration by Siddharth Chandra (now at Michigan State University), led within two years to a formal project for a world-historical dataset, labeled World-Historical Dataverse, with an accompanying website (WHD). This was then followed by an increasingly detailed collaboration of social scientists with the School of Information Science and with colleagues in the School of Public Health and the Department of Geology and Planetary Science. Visits by leading figures from Harvard, Portsmouth, and Microsoft Research advanced the discussion. Among those most active in Information Science were Dean Ronald Larsen, Geoffrey Bowker, Hassan Karimi, Vladimir Zadorozhny, and Stephen Hirtle. The biggest empirical step forward was a lively collaborative project linking disease surveillance data from the U.S. with overlapping climate data and population data: the cross-disciplinary collaboration was successful, though the empirical results were not imposing. The School of Arts and Sciences maintained its support for engagement of a post-doctoral fellow to support the World-Historical Dataverse project which was achieved in 2012 with the engagement of Kai Cao.[1] Dataverse meetings, held at the University of Pittsburgh, had implications at that campus and elsewhere. The 2011 meeting, an eclectic set of discussions, led to expanded work during the following year. Meetings in the following years took a different form as the broader CHIA project came to encompass the campus-based World-Historical Dataverse, which now became an element within CHIA.

The coalescence of CHIA in its present form came especially though work on a series of proposals for grants on global geographical and historical projects. A 2009 proposal submitted to the Mellon Foundation from Harvard University – on global historical GIS – included participation from the Center for Geographic Analysis (CGA), the Institute for Quantitative Social Science (IQSS), the CLIO project at Boston University, the University of Pittsburgh, the Human Relations Area Files (HRAF), the University of Portsmouth, and others. A 2010 proposal to the National Science Foundation – on global historical geographic ontology – included CGA, IQSS, CLIO, University of Texas-Austin, and

DOI: 10.1057/9781137378972

the World-Historical Dataverse (WHD). A 2011 proposal to the National Science Foundation from the University of Pittsburgh included CGA, IQSS, International Institute of Social History (IISH), Michigan State University, Portsmouth, and University of California-Merced. While none of these applications succeeded, the persistence and collaboration of the researchers provided a basis for the creation of CHIA in November 2011: its initial participants were WHD, CGA, IQSS, International Institute of Social History, and UC-Merced. Meetings at Pittsburgh in 2010, 2011, and 2012 included many of the leading participants, and the results set the stage for preparation of the 2012 application from the University of Pittsburgh to the National Science Foundation 'Building Community and Capacity' initiative, which was funded in 2012 for activity 2013–15.[2] A May 2013 meeting in Pittsburgh was the first full meeting of the CHIA group, focusing on the implementation of the NSF proposal but also addressing other dimensions of CHIA.

The organizational structure of CHIA was designed to fit its task. Administrative headquarters are at the University of Pittsburgh, where the project's objective had earlier gained recognition through university financial support. CHIA is housed in the World History Center, which was founded in 2008 as an institution for 'research, teaching, and international collaboration on the global past, with attention to policies for the global future' (WHC). Figure 3.1 indicates the structure of CHIA as it had expanded after two years of existence. The Headquarters office (at the University of Pittsburgh) and the Steering Committee, led by a director, coordinate the numerous projects. The Steering Committee meets twice a year: in person in Pittsburgh (in April) and in November by video conference. The CHIA Archive is formally under the direction of the Headquarters office and the Steering Committee: it is directed by an Archivist appointed by the Steering Committee. The founding and current archivist is Carlos Sanchez, who also serves as director of information for the School of Arts & Sciences at Pitt. In practice, the archive is widely distributed. It includes files at the Pittsburgh Supercomputer Center; files on a server at the School of Information Science at Pitt; files at the Harvard Dataverse Network; and other files that are held individually in expectation that they will be gradually submitted to one of the main repositories. The remaining element at the leadership level of CHIA is the *Journal of World-Historical Information*. This journal, founded in 2011 and first published in 2013, is intended to match the objectives of CHIA by attracting articles from a wide range of scholars

DOI: 10.1057/9781137378972

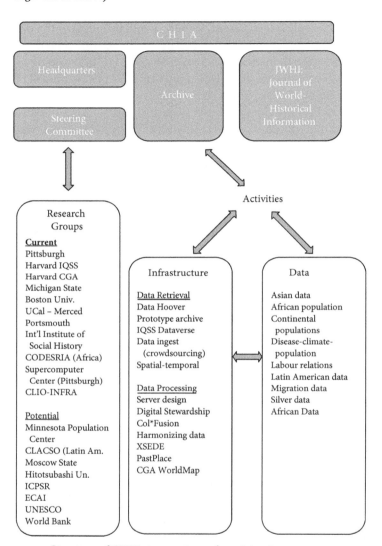

**FIGURE 3.1**    *Structure of CHIA: interactions of participating groups*

on the technical and interpretive issues in building a large-scale historical dataset. One of its most important contributions is expected to be the publication of peer reviews of published datasets, with the intention of attracting scholarly recognition to the important work of preparing fully documented historical datasets.

DOI: 10.1057/9781137378972

The lower section of Figure 3.1 displays a summary of CHIA's participating groups and their activities. In the left are the organizations that have been, formally, members of CHIA (at the top), and those that have maintained informal contacts or for which there are potential contacts (at the bottom). [3] In fact, the willingness of these groups to work together and their ability to find ways to advance the overall CHIA project has been remarkable.

Next, Figure 3.1 lists the current infrastructure tasks of the CHIA project. The actual tasks are described in detail in Chapters 4, 5, and 6. The quick summary here is to convey the process of organization of the work. The tasks include those of data retrieval – the 'data hoover' process, construction of a prototype archive, the interdisciplinary pilot dataset on disease, climate and population, the Spatio-Temporal Bridge for comparing datasets, and the CHIA crowdsourcing ingest system. Then come the tasks of data processing, including Digital Stewardship for data preservation, the Col*Fusion process of documentation, the XSEDE path to server design and high-speed processing, and the work on spatial documentation through PastPlace (NDSA, XSEDE, PastPlace). As the project develops, more effort will be put into modeling social scientific relationships, especially to simulate and otherwise estimate missing data. So far, an article in JWHI lays out a perspective on strategies for modeling across disciplinary lines, focusing on the recurring role of population variables in social science theories (Manning and Ravi 2013).

The final section of Figure 3.1 summarizes the tasks of data collection. The initial priority of CHIA is building a robust infrastructure for collecting, housing, and analyzing world-historical data, with NSF support. But this is not enough. The CHIA project cannot credibly proceed without demonstrating, in its early stages, the ability to collect large quantities of data. Not only must we find ways to collect large quantities of historical data, but we must establish relationships among the various topics, regions, and time periods inherent in the various datasets. Our work in this area has been without major funding, but it nonetheless includes several ongoing projects. Some of them are funded locally and others have been funded by awards to groups participating in CHIA. [4]

In the intermediate term, roughly five years, CHIA intends to develop a strong and expanding research team: it will unleash a rapid inflow of historical data to be documented and archived. CHIA will develop an overall ontology for world-historical documentation and analysis, including an expanding system of metadata to describe data and assist in

DOI: 10.1057/9781137378972

their integration and aggregation. CHIA will conduct interactive analysis at regional and global levels of variables in social sciences, health, and climate; and develop systems of visualization that will assist in analysis and provide feedback for collection and definition of data. Here are the goals for the five years beginning 2013:[5]

▸ Global Collaboration: collaborative relations to sustain and expand the creation of a world-historical data resource,
▸ Crowdsourcing applications: to facilitate data ingest,
▸ Col*Fusion: for file merging,
▸ CHIA Archive: a distributed archive with datasets held at five levels of integration into the overall CHIA system,
▸ Digital Stewardship: following best practices in housing and display of datasets,
▸ World-historical gazetteer: a comprehensive (though probably distributed) historical gazetteer, and a spatial search engine to accompany it,
▸ Temporal search engine: with extended temporal metadata,
▸ Ontology: a developing CHIA ontology, providing topical classification of data, as well as space, time, and the tasks and applications of CHIA,
▸ Data: energetic collection of historical data worldwide,
▸ Peer review: scholarly review of historical datasets to establish strong academic standards,
▸ Theory: engage debate on linkage of social science theories to each other.

Of these, we have made a good start in global collaboration and in our crowdsourcing application. The CHIA archive will be tested as more data come in: we have access to the facilities of the Pittsburgh Supercomputing Center (PSC). Crowdsourcing and peer-reviewing may spread beyond the CHIA project: in addition to satisfying the needs of the CHIA project, we hope that achieving these goals will also help to spread benefits more broadly through social scientific analysis. Most important, however, is the basic objective: since we have now become fully cognizant of the global nature of human society – by which we mean the intensity of global social interactions and the interactions of the human and natural world – it is a top priority for us to learn about the historical record, at regional and global levels, of our evolving human society. Based on the unfolding results

DOI: 10.1057/9781137378972

of the first five years, CHIA's leadership is already beginning to envision priorities for work at a subsequent stage.

The CHIA program of activity relies on an underlying philosophy which emphasizes a consistently global vision, combined with intensive interactions at local and intermediate levels. This global vision ensures that overall project strategy remains fixed on developing world-historical data on human society – even though details of the project may sometimes distract researchers from the big picture. To implement this global strategy, the project emphasizes building a research collaborative that balances the autonomy of affiliates with the coordination of communication and decision-making through headquarters. Headquarters is the center of gravity, maintaining the archive and facilitating communication. The affiliates are institutionally based groups of researchers – researchers who carry out the tasks of data collection, documentation, and analysis, commonly in collaboration with each other. Participating groups include three or more researchers, based at a research institution, who propose and submit deliverables; they are otherwise self-governing or governed by their local institutions. In addition, individual researchers may become participants in CHIA by agreeing to submit historical data. The CHIA collaborative is to facilitate the sharing of data by individual researchers through crowdsourcing and analysis of the archival holdings by individuals and groups; it is also to ensure broad participation in the making and review of key decisions.

CHIA emphasizes cross-disciplinary alliances in academic fields: this means close, research-focused relationships among researchers of distinct social science fields and equally close work with researchers in natural science fields and in information science. All of these cross-disciplinary links support the development of a project to link and unify social science theory, both to expand the realm of theory and to advance the collection, estimation, and analysis of social science data. Of central importance is CHIA's commitment to open access: free access to its materials, emphasizing the participation of researchers, teachers, and students, who will be able to consult data, use the project's visualization tools, and conduct data analyses at every stage of the project.

The range of tasks and activities carried out under the umbrella of CHIA is complex. Equally complex is the range of governance and reporting systems accompanying the projects. Funded projects require reports to the funding agency and demonstration of adequate oversight in project activity. Unfunded activities, sometimes central to CHIA's overall

DOI: 10.1057/9781137378972

plan, require support from the Steering Committee and project staff. The overall CHIA organization chart needs to be updated as activities begin and end, and it needs to be interpreted flexibly at any moment.

## Techniques of collaboration: participants and headquarters

For CHIA to accomplish its missions of data-gathering, aggregation, and analysis – and thereby to provide answers to big questions on the global dynamics of social change – it must create a suitable cyber infrastructure and a coherent stream of data. In terms of a recent initiative of the National Science Foundation of the U.S., completing each mission requires 'building community and capacity for data-intensive research'.[6] The criteria for the overall infrastructure are *analytical* – this is the capacity side of the CHIA mission: i) the data repository must be able to store spatial and temporal attributes flexibly to capture changes in borders and a variety of time scales; ii) organizing the data requires estimating large amounts of missing data and transforming data for consistency; iii) processing of data will benefit greatly from existing and new data-mining methods; iv) analysis requires linking of disparate theories; and v) visualization requires conveying analytical results and displaying elements of large data sets at various temporal and spatial scales.

The infrastructure criteria are also *organizational* – that is, the collaboration side of the CHIA mission: i) the Collaborative must achieve a readiness to contribute data among social, health, and environmental scientists; ii) researchers must cooperate in maintaining high and consistent standards in documenting data; and iii) theorists in various fields must collaborate to link their models. The need to work simultaneously and collaboratively on these issues helps explain why the Collaborative has taken form.[7]

The following chapters address the work of CHIA in terms of three missions. At the same time, while the three missions are distinct, the task of creating global historical data requires constant interaction and feedback among the various parts of the project. For instance, in one sense the visualization and analysis of data come, logically, after the collection of data. On the other hand, the results of analysis and visualization will provide new ideas on what data are most important and how they should be defined – so that the needs of analysis help determine what

DOI: 10.1057/9781137378972

data should be collected and estimated. Similarly, the assembly of data that have already been archived into regional and global aggregations of evidence comes logically after the collection of data. On the other hand, one needs a sense of which types of global historical data will be most valuable in analysis in order to set priorities for collecting the localized datasets which are to be the building blocks.

As director of the CHIA project, I have found it exciting to learn elements of all the types of data and technologies involved in this process. But I don't know and probably cannot know details of all the processes, and I sometimes make mistakes in understanding where the details fit in. In fact, much of my work has consisted of working to get relevant people together in meetings, and to stand back and see what innovative steps they propose. On the other hand, it has been my privilege to be in contact with almost every dimension of the project and to see how they fit together. Occasionally I have been able to identify gaps in the logic of the project that require new activities; I have joined with others in determining the priorities and sequence of activities and in working endlessly on honing overall project terminology and the linkages of the various activities. One could not claim that project participants have had no conflicts, yet the overall atmosphere has been one of remarkable and enthusiastic openness and collaboration across disciplinary and institutional lines. Participants have worked energetically and imaginatively on identifying and resolving many successive problems in design and execution. Contacts among our participating groups have been most intensive when we are focusing on meeting the deadline for submission of a major grant proposal. Email and especially conference telephone calls reaching over nine time zones have been the basis for confirming our consensus.

How are we to retain the basis for such close work in times between grant proposals? One technique we have used is that of inviting groups to become formal participants in CHIA. (University lawyers won't let us use the term 'members' because CHIA is not a legally constituted body.) Announcing formal participation is perhaps too simple, especially if we are not asking for membership fees. So, in addition, CHIA has asked each of its participants to identify and submit a formal 'deliverable' each within  six months. The actual deliverables might be datasets or data definition criteria, or they might be a more basic agreement to provide consultation services (for instance, on GIS) to participants throughout CHIA. Every six months, CHIA is expected to review the deliverables

DOI: 10.1057/9781137378972

received from each participating organization. Because of the many other activities underway at each campus, deliverables do not always arrive on time. Nonetheless, having the procedure in place helps to sustain a sense of shared work linking all of the groups that participate in CHIA.

The CHIA headquarters is a small office, consisting of the director and an administrative staff person. One might hope for the development of an office routine, but in fact the needs of the moment shift regularly, so that the headquarters must mostly work on new questions. Still, the main priority is that of maintaining contact with all participating groups and working to facilitate their connections with each other. The number of participating groups around the world is expected to rise steadily, and the demands for effective coordination at headquarters will rise accordingly. Among the means of communication are periodic newsletters and video conferences – either for individuals involved in a specific process or for gathering large numbers of CHIA participants for a general question-and-answer session.

To summarize, CHIA will create an infrastructure for retrieving, holding, and analyzing world-historical data. CHIA will be an institution of sufficient scale and authority to address the analytical and organizational challenges of documenting human society in recent centuries. It will develop new data standards that account for heterogeneity, procedures for documenting and integrating heterogeneous data, and permanent housing for both raw and transformed data. It will facilitate cross-disciplinary analysis and visualization, sustaining synergies among researchers in social, health, environmental, and information sciences. It will lead to elaboration of theory to connect existing theories. In organizational terms, CHIA will facilitate a campaign encouraging social scientists to collect and submit historical data for shared access and analysis. Out of this campaign there may arise an improved system of reward and recognition for sharing data. The Collaborative will lead in articulating good practice in the inevitable debates about the ownership of data and citation and recognition of the contributors of data.

This is by no means the first effort to assemble historical social science data on a large scale. The CHIA group is aware of the challenges, achievements, and failures of earlier groups. For instance, systems of national income accounting – established for most major national economies in post-war years – stand as an immense achievement in research, accounting, and analysis. These national accounts were created not only for current years but for past years, going back generations. On the other hand,

DOI: 10.1057/9781137378972

current and retrospective national income accounts were calculated for some nations and not for others, and those without such data remain deprived in economic analysis and policy. Such historical data collection and analysis is in many ways parallel to the project we are now taking on – except that ours is at least an order of magnitude larger in scale .

Attention to past projects brings forth one more lesson in collaborative behavior for CHIA. That is, CHIA must remain ready to change its organization and update its technology in order to remain on the cutting edge of building large-scale datasets. Too often, projects fall into a sort of tunnel vision that relies on certain initial choices: they fail to put forth the energy to revise their priorities in order to broaden and update the results of their work. We return to this issue in Chapter 7. For now, the point is that CHIA must be prepared to shift its approach repeatedly in order to stay on the path toward achieving its primary goal, creating an effective world-historical data resource.

## The need for participants in the CHIA project

For historians, social scientists, and policymakers, the objective is to convey the notion that a world-historical archive is valuable, feasible, and that we urge them to contribute data available to them. This book argues that archiving and aggregating local data can lead to large-scale and even global collections of data, in which one can gain a sense of the global without losing touch with the local and with intermediate levels of human experience. For information scientists, I emphasize that the project is feasible though challenging, and that they are invited to contribute their skills and insights to its construction. For natural scientists, work with CHIA provides access to linked data on natural and human processes, and permits exploration over time of the human–natural interactions that are now a central issue in research. The work is intricate and complex, but newly developed collaborative techniques permit the creation of such a valuable archive. For humanities scholars, it is important that they realize that the long-term plan of the world-historical archive is to include textual and visual information and not just quantitative data in tabular form. Texts and images can be linked to the archive by time and place, and can then be mined and analyzed to reveal the outlooks and opinions of authors at many stages in history, and thus prepare for

DOI: 10.1057/9781137378972

the analysis of the past (from local to global) through many different perspectives.

In this appeal to potential collaborators, a key emphasis is the project's careful balance among its dimensions. For instance, on one hand the project must be open and decentralized in encouraging participants to submit data and develop procedures of interest to them; on the other hand the project must maintain central control of consolidating and aggregating files in order to create valid global summaries. Similarly, the archive must be responsive to and protective of the work of individual contributors in a bottom-up approach to archiving; at the same time, it must generate an overall ontology and a comprehensive archive at the global level. This social scientific world-historical archive will be rather different from the global climate models now in use, but in fact the global climate models provide the closest parallel to the world-historical archive, and we will explore those parallels in detail.

# Notes

1   Dr. Cao's position is supported by the Dietrich School of Arts and Sciences at the University of Pittsburgh. In addition, the Office of the Provost at Pitt provided grants of US$ 40,000 to the World-Historical Dataverse during 2011–12 and 2012–13.

2   Full records of the Pittsburgh WHD workshops of 23 February 2011 and 27 March 2012, including videotaped presentations and slides, are available online at www.dataverse.pitt.edu/announcements/feb2011workshop.php and www.dataverse.pitt.edu/announcements/mar2012colloquium.php, respectively.

3   Research groups participating in CHIA as of September 2013:
    University of Pittsburgh (faculty members and research associates in World History Center, Global Studies, Geology, Public Health, and Information Science; graduate assistants.
    Institute for Quantitative Social Science, Harvard University (one faculty member and three research associates)
    Center for Geographic Analysis, Harvard University (two research associates)
    University of California – Merced (one faculty member, graduate researcher)
    Michigan State University (one faculty member, two research associates)
    CLIO, Boston University (one faculty member, one research associate)
    International Institute for Social History, Amsterdam (two faculty members, two research associates)

DOI: 10.1057/9781137378972

Portsmouth University (one faculty member, two research associates)

CLIO-INFRA, International Institute for Social History (one faculty member, one research associate)

Council for the Development of Economic and Social Research in Africa (CODESRIA) (Executive Secretary and one research associateo

Research groups with which CHIA has informal contacts in September 2013

Consejo Latinoamericano de Ciencias Sociales (CLACSO), Buenos Aires

Faculty of Global Studies, Lomonosov Moscow State University

Economic History, Hitotsubashi University

Minnesota Population Center

Electronic Cultural Atlas Initiative

4   Data collection activities are identified, directed, and located as follows:

Asian Data. S. Chandra, Michigan State University.

African Population. P. Manning, Pitt.

Disease-Climate-Demography. W. van Panhuis, D. Bain, Pitt.

Global Collaboratory on Labour Relations. U. Bosma and K. Hofmeester, IISH.

Migration Data proposal. U. Bosma, IISH.

Silver Data. P. Manning, Pitt.

African Data. E. Sall, CODESRIA.

Continental Populations. P. Manning, Pitt; R. Zijdeman, IISH.

Religion Data. R. Woodberry, Singapore.

Contemporary global data. A. Karatayev, Moscow State U.

Economic history data. Hitotsubashi U.

5   The same priorities for the first five years are summarized again in Chapter 8, but condensed to five categories.

6   National Science Foundation, 'Building Community and Capacity for Data-Intensive Research in the Social, Behavioral, and Economic Sciences and in Education and Human Resources (BCC-SBE/EHR)', program announcement NSF 12–538. http://www.nsf.gov/pubs/2012/nsf12538/nsf12538.htm.

7   U.S. National Science Foundation awards to CHIA for Building Capacity and Community (BCC, September 2012): awards 1244282, 1244667, 1244672, 1244693, 1244796.

DOI: 10.1057/9781137378972

# 4

# Mission 1: Assembling and Documenting the Data

**Abstract:** *Historical data, often of great value, lie widely dispersed and in inconsistent forms – previously inaccessible and unreadable. Digitization projects have begun to process historical data, and CHIA provides a way to coordinate this work. Print resources such as the British Parliamentary Papers and archival records from Lisbon, Rome, and Beijing await inclusion. The crowdsourcing infrastructure, Col\*Fusion, may be a great step forward in linking datasets. The Col\*Fusion process records data plus detailed metadata on source, place, time, specifics of the topic, and on modifications to the data. Each dataset, as incorporated, benefits from a program of digital stewardship, carefully preserving it and ensuring that users of a dataset will cite the author.*

**Keywords:** crowdsourcing; digital stewardship; digitization; historical data; metadata

Manning, Patrick. *Big Data in History*. Basingstoke: Palgrave Macmillan, 2013. DOI: 10.1057/9781137378972.

DOI: 10.1057/9781137378972

Mission 1 is to gather, archive, and document historical data. The collaborative dimension of this mission focuses especially on data collection but also on data documentation. The chapter is divided into five sections, each rather different from the other, which combine to create the basic organization and content of the CHIA Archive. First is the issue of identifying the relevant historical data to be included in the archive. Manuscript, print, and digital data have all to be gathered and submitted to CHIA. Second is the ingest of data into the CHIA Level 1 Archive through the crowdsourcing system. The ingested datasets include those prepared by scholars in the CHIA project but also those submitted by many others, relying on a crowdsourcing infrastructure. Upon ingest, the datasets are reviewed and sorted into various sections of the Level 1 Archive. The result is a large number of parallel datasets, as submitted by their creators, which are sustained by the system of Digital Stewardshop. These Level 1 datasets may be analyzed and visualized by users, for instance through the Spatio-Temporal Bridge.

The third section of the chapter focuses on data integration – in effect, the merging of datasets. Col*Fusion is the infrastructure developed at the University of Pittsburgh which permits the integration of datasets through identifying variables that are common to two or more datasets, and then expanding steadily the degree of integration among the linked datasets. The datasets that have gone through the Col*Fusion process are held in the Level 2 CHIA Archive.

The fourth section of the chapter addresses the standards for consistent documentation of the files held within Level 2. These standards, which begin with those developed in the succeeding iterations of the Data Documentation Initiative, address the data sources plus documentation of space, time, topics, and scale of the variables and observations within each dataset. The fifth section of the chapter returns to the issue of analysis and visualization, and discusses how these activities can be carried out for files at each level of the archive.

## Identifying relevant historical data

Which data are to be included? For this initial large-scale effort at creating a global historical dataset, we need to be at once wide-ranging and selective in identifying data for inclusion: wide-ranging because we don't know in advance which data will work out best; selective because we

DOI: 10.1057/9781137378972

want to focus our efforts and develop an initial version that can reach an advanced stage fairly soon so that we can revise, reformulate, and expand. The initial work of data collection focuses especially on aspects of population. Population records come from formal censuses, from local and religious censuses, and from military records. Trade data are available from port records, from commercial tax registers, and from the records of individual business firms. Money supplies and money flows can be documented from commercial records. Climate data, directly measured by instruments for recent times, can also be indirectly measured by recent geological research. Valuable and accessible health data include accounts of epidemic disease and studies of death rates. Other relevant data include food production, trade, and consumption; social data on births, marriages, deaths, and communities; religious records on individuals and groups; and reports of travelers. Most of the data mentioned here are quantitative, but qualitative data – in text and images – also have value. These qualitative data can be archived and described by time, place, author and other descriptive information; procedures of data mining can then extract patterns from the data.

## Manuscript data

In addition to published data, and especially for earlier times, the majority of the historical data we seek is in manuscript form – handwritten documents located in archives. The most convenient of such data are located in well-run archives of national governments or great institutions: in Britain, France, the Netherlands, Russia, Japan, China, Turkey, Mexico, and in the archives of the Catholic Church, especially in Rome. Private archival data exist in manuscript form in the records of businesses or individuals or social institutions. Even more data are held by families: in an extraordinary instance, families in and around the fabled West African city of Timbuktu, in recent years, donated great quantities of previously hidden historical documents, mostly in Arabic language, which have since been placed in regional archives for preservation, digitization, and historical analysis (Tombouctou Manuscripts Project). Digitization may require manual or mechanical entry to turn manuscript into digital files, and special work to digitize tabular data. To demonstrate that this work is feasible, one may turn to the case of the work done by David Eltis, who read through the Foreign Office archives in London and found the detailed reports of surveillance of slave trade

DOI: 10.1057/9781137378972

throughout the Atlantic. He transcribed and then digitized the data, then added them to a general database. His results, now digitized and published as part of the Slave Voyages database, provided important new results – that the Atlantic slave trade of the nineteenth century, though at that point 'illegal', continued at the same rate as in the eighteenth century until it halted just after 1850 (Eltis 1981, Eltis 2010). Christian religious censuses, both Catholic and Protestant, add much data. Levels of uncertainty in these data need to be identified. Data can come from transcription or perhaps scanning of handwritten administrative records accumulated over hundreds of years in the imperial archives in Beijing, Istanbul, or Lisbon. Such important work raises the problem of the high cost of transcription, digitization, and verification of historical data. Yet while the cost of this work is high, the value of the data may be even higher.

## Print data

One massive category of historical data consists of information that has been published but not digitized in searchable form. From the early nineteenth century, many governments published annual records on trade, taxation, and government expenditure. Newspapers published clearings and arrivals of ships. Such documents are available not only for western Europe but for Russia, Japan, Latin American countries, the Ottoman Empire, and for European colonies in all parts of the world. In some cases electronic records have been made of these documents in the form of PDF files, but PDF files do not generally enable searching on individual characters on each page. Scanning through Optical Character Recognition (OCR) can be used to digitize such printed files, though the accuracy of OCR is not yet high enough to provide dependable results on quantitative data. It is possible that a procedure involving multiple OCR files of each page, with comparison of the results, will enable automatic digitization of print data files. An outstanding example of published data that could be incorporated in CHIA comes from the British Parliamentary Papers for the nineteenth and early twentieth century. These extensive publications document society, economy, and government for Britain and the British Empire, and also for regions throughout the world, providing broad and systematic data on trade and government finance, on migration and other aspects of population. Data can come from the incorporation of thousands of pages of tables on

DOI: 10.1057/9781137378972

trade and administration of units worldwide as published in the British Parliamentary Papers from 1801.[1] Similarly, commercial and other data published in newspapers, in many languages, add substantially to the available data.

## Privately held scholarly datasets

A large, heterogeneous, and important reservoir of historical data consists of the datasets created and held by thousands of individual historians who have collected, organized, and documented historical data on topics of their interest. Commonly they publish portions of the data along with historical interpretations based on the data, but the full datasets remain unpublished. The CHIA Archive is proposed as a safe haven for these datasets, in which they can be preserved and made available to the scholarly community generally, while ensuring proper citation of them by users. Another dimension of data collection is the system to facilitate incorporation of data brought by researchers who wish to submit data they have developed, documented, and perhaps analyzed. For this task we are investing substantial energy in developing a 'crowdsourcing' application that enables remote users to interact with the archive, enter the documentation for their data, and then submit the data. (As noted, these datasets can go through the Col*Fusion process either following pre-processing in Level 1 Archive, or directly from contributor to Col*Fusion if the data are clean and well documented.)

## Existing large-scale datasets

With the recent advances in technology, many scholars have been developing large-scale historical datasets on various topics. These datasets represent some of the best new work in historical studies, and their implications for future advances in research are substantial. The datasets focus on populations (slave and free), shipping, trade, labor, prices, and other factors (Eltis 2010, Sound Toll, CLIO-INFRA, NHGIS, GBHGIS). Yet each of them is organized as a discrete dataset, so that there has been little progress in locating the links among them. The potential of CHIA is that data from these discrete datasets can be ingested and integrated into the CHIA Archive, thus permitting the exploration of interactions among the various frontiers of historical research.

DOI: 10.1057/9781137378972

## A culture of data-sharing

Commonly, however, social science scholars remain reluctant to share or publish the historical datasets that they have constructed with such care. What is needed is a change in the values and professional practices of scholars. That is, they should agree to submit systematically the data they collect to publicly available repositories where others can check their work and can use the same resources for additional research. Efforts to develop such data-sharing practices have been carried out for generations, some of them with remarkable success, as in the Human Relations Area Files created by anthropologists (HRAF). For the most part, however, such efforts have advanced only slowly among historians and other social scientists.

# CHIA activities for data retrieval (Level 1 Archive)

Participants in the CHIA collaborative include historians who have worked energetically in all aspects of constructing and archiving historical datasets. Their data range across African commerce and population, social history of colonial Louisiana, studies of opium and influenza in British India, administrative decisions in Song China, British labor history, religious censuses, and a wide-ranging study of colonialism. To advance the study of their own data, these scholars are contributing to CHIA and working to build and analyze the Archive.

## Disease – climate – population

The World-Historical Dataverse has been able to join with the Graduate School of Public Health at Pitt in a collaborative project to explore the limits of cross-disciplinary research, in large part to demonstrate the feasibility of the larger CHIA project. The key element of the collaboration is Project Tycho™, a project of the School of Public Health which has located, digitized, and built a massive dataset consisting of the United States weekly reports of disease surveillance (by city or county) for the whole period from 1888 to 2011 (TYCHO).[2] It is a remarkable example of 'data rescue', to use the term of Donald Burke, Project Tycho™ director and Dean of the School of Public Health. The dataset is of immense importance in the historical understanding of disease: it shows the changes in principal diseases with time, the discovery of new

DOI: 10.1057/9781137378972

diseases, the effects of vaccines, and also the changing administrative systems for collecting disease data.

To initiate cross-disciplinary research, Burke suggested, in late 2010, the linkage of disease data with data on climate and population. By mid-2011 a small research team had formed: Wilbert van Panhuis of Public Health, who had done much of the work on Project Tycho™; Daniel J. Bain, a climatologist from the Department of Geology and Planetary Science; and graduate students able to work with population data.[3] The researchers chose to focus on measles and polio cases in eastern cities of the United States. They made substantial progress in linking the three types of data together and developed 'heat maps' as an elegant form of visualizing changes in disease over space and time. While no strong analytical results arose in the short term, the project was immensely beneficial to the coalescence of CHIA. It developed practice in cross-disciplinary collaboration among the researchers, it strengthened the experience of the World History Center in funding and administering the project, and it led to new hypotheses on relations of disease and climate. While the work was limited to a national scale within the U.S., it conveyed important elements of a global analysis.[4]

## Data hoover

How is the CHIA project to acquire datasets? CHIA seeks at once to survey social scientists about the datasets they hold and to identify techniques for encouraging them to submit copies of their datasets to archives. This is the 'data-hoover' project, referring to a human analog of the Hoover vacuum cleaner, intended to draw in all of the available historical data. This project, considered for years, was launched in 2013 under the leadership of Ruth Mostern at the University of California – Merced. Initially, the 'data-hoover' researcher, Marieka Arksey, is to survey faculty members at one or more universities, to identify the amount of historical data that are held by various researchers – and, hopefully, to learn of techniques for encouraging researchers to submit copies of their data to a general repository. As the project expands, it may be possible to appoint a 'data-hoover' at the senior level: that is, an academic diplomat who meets with editors of journals and officers of professional associations, to encourage them to require that authors of published articles submit the data to back up the arguments of their articles. Such a requirement has already been established by the *American Economic*

DOI: 10.1057/9781137378972

*Review*, and the CLIO-INFRA research group has been circulating, among economic historians, a proposed Policy on Data Availability with the same objective.

## Prototype global dataset

The prototype global dataset is a small-scale example of a systematic global historical dataset. It is to provide experience in working with global historical parameters and to verify the feasibility of documenting and analyzing data at a global scale. The study includes four types of historical variables, documented for all regions of the world and for most of the twentieth century. The data include populations at national levels and (for very populous nations) at provincial levels; periodic climate conditions for identified places and times within the same spatial units; basic statistics on wars of the twentieth century; and silver flows in production and trade. The result is a relational dataset including tables for each of the varying types of data. The accompanying metadata comprise a system of data documentation that enables all the variables to be aggregated and compared – including, for instance, elements of a global time register. Work on this project advanced substantially during 2013 thanks to the efforts of Chelsea Mafrica, a computer science graduate student at Pitt. The prototype dataset will continue to be developed and analyzed; in addition, it has been incorporated into the CHIA Archive through Col*Fusion.

## Crowdsourcing for data ingest

In previous efforts to gather large quantities of data, the bottleneck has been the limits on the willingness and ability of researchers to submit their data to a common repository. Important and valuable initiatives such as the Electronic Cultural Atlas Initiative and ChronoZoom have fallen short of their targets in collecting data for lack of a means to open this bottleneck (ChronoZoom, ECAI). When explored in detail, the bottleneck in data submission turns out to result both from the outlook of researchers and the inherent difficulties of completing and conveying historical datasets. The researchers have concerns about the impermanence of online resources, about recognition and citation of their work – they find that the academic world gives little recognition either to the cost or the value of historical datasets. Those who do seek to submit data find that the submission process is complex and that the data, once submitted, are difficult for users to find.

DOI: 10.1057/9781137378972

Crowdsourcing has developed recently both as a technology and as a philosophy of collective intelligence. As a technology, crowdsourcing uses online interfaces with public access to gather and exchange information. One major success in use of this technique is the Galaxy Zoo, in which amateur astronomers, working with online images, completed typological descriptions of thousands of galaxies with unexpected rapidity (GALAXY ZOO). As a philosophy of collective intelligence, crowdsourcing works by decentering research and relying on widely dispersed knowledge. The shift to an approach based on collective intelligence involves a major reorganization of the work style of historians and other scholars – more time listening to others and more time explaining things to others. The result, however, may have the benefit of engaging the expert knowledge of historians, now dispersed among individuals, and focusing it on building a collaborative resource. In a real sense, the world-historical data resource now under construction reflects the collaboration that was necessary to sustain, in the past, the societies that historians now analyze.

Continuing effort is required to ensure that the crowdsourcing device conveys an attractive interface to users: it must provide contributors with considerable practical benefits in order to attract them. We are hopeful, however, that we can develop a successful and user-friendly interface. The users we expect to attract are drawn from the many experienced historians, both professional and amateur, who are skilled in the domain knowledge of the many subfields of history and are devoted to collection and study of data.

Within the CHIA group, Vladimir Zadorozhny championed the idea of a crowdsourcing approach to ingest. From Fall 2011 he worked with several graduate students in developing initial stages of an interface through which remote users could submit datasets in detail to a repository. By spring 2012 the idea had developed sufficiently that it was written up as a central element of the group's major proposal to NSF. With the award from NSF, full-scale work began at the start of 2013 and by July 2013 – thanks especially to the work of doctoral student Evgeny Karataev – a working version of the CHIA crowdsourcing data-ingest system had been implemented and tested. Research groups that had long been associated with CHIA now found contributing their data to the larger study more convenient, and began to submit significant segments of their own data to the CHIA Level 1 Archive, though they continued to keep copies on their local servers.

DOI: 10.1057/9781137378972

This architecture efficiently combines methods of crowdsourcing with wrapper/mediator technology. We assume that information providers will submit wrappers that utilize an application programming interface (API) to extract information from their corresponding data sources and to map the information to a standard homogeneous representation. The crowdsourcing data-ingest site became available to the research public just as this book was going into production, through the CHIA website (CHIA). In fact the data-ingest site is very closely tied to Col*Fusion, the system for consistent documentation of newly ingested data, but there is a benefit to distinguishing the two initial steps for purposes of this presentation. It is the difference between files held in the CHIA Level 1 Archive and the CHIA Level 2 Archive.

## Review of ingested datasets

This is the process of evaluation of each dataset, by CHIA staff, as it enters the CHIA system. Each dataset is reviewed for consistency of the type and formatting of data, and for the detail and consistency of metadata. The review includes recommendations on the next steps for each incoming file. First, a copy of every incoming file goes to the Base Archive within Level 1. Second, files may go to pre-processing for cleaning and upgrading of metadata, so that they will be ready for incorporation either into the Spatio-Temporal Bridge or the Col*Fusion process.

## Base archive

The CHIA crowdsourcing data-ingest site – that is, the CHIA Level 1 Archive – provides a straightforward system by which contributors of datasets may archive their datasets, documenting them according to their own preferences (within the confines of some basic rules). In that sense it is comparable to the archive of the Interuniversity Consortium on Political and Social Research (ICPSR) and to the Dataverse Network Archive. In sum, the CHIA Level 1 Archive is a repository at which individual datasets may be housed and maintained permanently; it facilitates their use and citation by researchers. In addition, files in the Level 1 archive are on a path of pre-processing that can lead them to more thorough incorporation into Level 2 of the CHIA archive. Further, CHIA Level 1 files benefit from CHIA's Digital Stewardship program for maintaining and distributing datasets.

DOI: 10.1057/9781137378972

In fact, this archive has existed since 2009. Founded as the World-Historical Dataverse archive, it began as data files prepared at the University of Pittsburgh and other datasets submitted to the WHD project, yet stored at DVN at Harvard and also accessible through WHD at Pitt.[5] The bottleneck for the WHD project, as for others, was the difficulty of arranging for digitization of additional data and the difficulty of arranging for scholars to submit their datasets.

## Col*Fusion and collective intelligence (moving to Level 2 Archive)

Finally, ingested datasets can be directed from Level 1 to the Col*Fusion application, either initially or after pre-processing. This is the most direct extension of the crowdsourcing data-ingest, and it leads to comprehensive documentation and merging of datasets. We assume that, at the earlier stage of ingest, contributors have submitted wrappers that utilize an application programming interface (API) to extract metadata information from their corresponding data sources and to map the information to a standard homogeneous representation of data documentation. If the data set includes information not covered by a target schema, we extend the schema correspondingly. The data submission system allows providers to register their wrappers as a part of the data-access layer of the global repository. The system also supports a wrapper-generation functionality to facilitate the wrapper development process. The wrappers can be used either to access data remotely or to load or replicate parts of the data at different nodes of the distributed repository. As we will see, reliance on crowdsourcing brings benefits not only for data ingest but also for data documentation and data-reliability assessment.

Figure 4.1 displays the steps of Mission 1. The initial steps of Mission 1 are shown at the upper left, where contributors submit data through the crowdsourcing system of data ingest. All incoming datasets are preserved in the Base (or Level 1) Archive, through the practice of Digital Stewardship. Some datasets may need pre-processing; others will be ready to enter directly into Col*Fusion. The Col*Fusion application ensures a consistent documentation of each new file with metadata on source, content, time, and space. Completion of these steps through Col*Fusion creates a CHIA dataset to be housed in the Level 2 Archives. Recurring merging of CHIA datasets leads to new and expanded CHIA

DOI: 10.1057/9781137378972

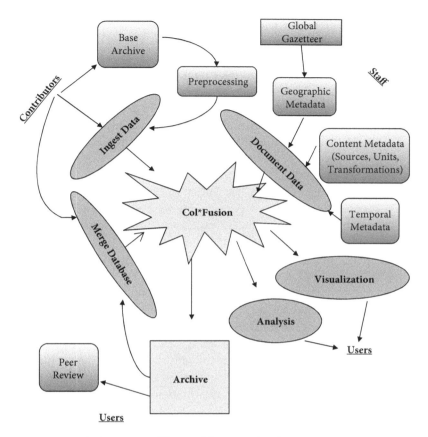

**FIGURE 4.1**    *Mission 1: assembling and documenting data*

datasets. Indeed, perhaps the most important achievement of Col*Fusion will be that of file-merging. The merging of files has previously been possible only when their data-description formats were identical, *ex ante*. With Col*Fusion it becomes possible to merge files once they share one or two similarly constituted variables. The importance of this merging of files *within* CHIA will become evident as we explore further steps. In addition, however, the Col*Fusion procedure may have important implications *beyond* CHIA. That is, if implemented independently by researchers, the Col*Fusion application may permit the merging of large numbers of files relevant to research projects that have previously been hindered by having to work with discrete files.[6]

DOI: 10.1057/9781137378972

Discussion continues within the CHIA project as to the distinction between CHIA crowdsourcing ingest and Col*Fusion integration. The two were conceptualized together, as a system bringing in data and linking files together with a common, 'targeted schema' of metadata. But as these steps came to be set in the context of the full CHIA project, intervening steps began to appear. That is, it became clear that the potential attractiveness of CHIA as a repository for historical data might be a separate issue from the full integration of datasets into a combined repository. Some datasets, once submitted, might require considerable cleaning and other pre-processing before they could be put into the Col*Fusion process. Further, the labor involved in determining specific metadata for variables – conceivably for numerous variables – in Col*Fusion might dampen the enthusiasm of some researchers as they submit their datasets.

As a result, a need emerged to establish the stage to 'review ingested datasets' immediately after ingest. Here the CHIA staff assesses the readiness of files for incorporation through Col*Fusion, the degree of pre-processing necessary, and the preferences of the contributors on whether their datasets should go simply to the Base Archive, and whether they should go to the Spatio-Temporal Bridge. Nevertheless, the path from data ingest to Col*Fusion remains the golden road for incoming data, and it is hoped that a high proportion of data contributions will follow that route. But for now, at least, fitting the two crowdsourcing steps into a fuller path of review and alternative destinations for incoming datasets is most appropriate for enabling CHIA to grow to the maximum in providing a range of contributions toward the creation of world-historical data.

## Standards for data documentation (basic metadata in Level 2 Archive)

For all evidence being submitted to the Level 2 Archive, it is necessary to document the data fully and also to verify the consistency and accuracy of the data. The 'metadata' – the statements of data description – must fully define the source of each dataset, the creator or compiler of the data, and the precise definition of each variable and each value. Of particular importance is the attribution of source, ownership and compilation of data, as the project seeks to maintain complete and accurate attribution,

DOI: 10.1057/9781137378972

not only for each dataset submitted by a contributor but also for all the derivative datasets incorporating materials from that dataset. For the assessment of data reliability, both CHIA contributors and users will be able to submit their subjective data-reliability assessments through an online interface. These are *external* reliability assessments which will be combined with *internal* reliability assessment protocols based on analysis of data inconsistencies in the integrated repositories. The data-reliability assessment will be a part of the process of data curation (Digital Stewardship) and data fusion.

One can expect that most data submitted to the CHIA project will come in the form of electronic spreadsheets. But in addition to the values in the cells there is need for specific definition of each of the variables and a considerably fuller list of documentation of each dataset and its data. In sum this corresponds to the metadata or data documentation. Researchers in quantitative social science have developed a succession of standards providing the specific organization and extent of data documentation: the Dublin Core and the Data Documentation Initiative (versions 1, 2, and 3) are key examples (DCMI, DDI). These data standards provide information on the sources and compilers of data. In addition, to achieve interconnection of historical datasets around the world, the metadata must provide consistent descriptions of the places and times to which data refer. Metadata can be at the level of the data file, at the level of variables within a dataset, or at the level of individual observations or cells, and must be structured and stored differently at each of these levels. (The most basic such metadata will be verified or added at Level 2; fuller documentation takes place at Level 3.)

Here is some additional detail on the underlying nature of data documentation. One important point to start with is that the metadata must be linked to or even part of the dataset itself. The overriding rule is that each data value within a dataset must be fully defined in terms of its source, its dimensions, and any transformations or aggregations it has undergone between its original source and its current position in the dataset. Consider the simplest case, the addition of a single number. At least four pieces of information need to be added beyond the number itself: *what* is being measured; *where* the information or reporting unit is located; *when* (date or period); and the *source* of information (including the contributor). To hold this information in a consistent structure, answers to these questions need to be selected from controlled vocabularies (sets of predefined terms – though these can be extended by users). The controlled vocabulary for *where* would be a gazetteer or GIS, though it would have to account for variations in boundaries and labels of locations; an analogous and flexible vocabulary is needed for *when*. The controlled vocabulary for *what* is the most challenging, as there is no established thesaurus for statistical concepts, although classifications have been developed for occupations and diseases.

This and other stages of documentation are contributions to the overall ontology – the overarching classification system – of the global archive. Various aspects of the ontology are established at different stages of the project. Initially it includes what we here call metadata – the description of values and variables in each data set and the recording of the sources and compilers of data. The incorporation of such existing detailed classifications means that data-ingest work can start before the high level framework – the overall project ontology – is finalized. Later stages of ontology include more comprehensive categorization of types of data, definitions and classification for the linkage and aggregation of datasets, and definitions for the analysis and visualization of data.

## Preliminary analysis and visualization (Archive Levels 1 and 2)

To succeed in building the CHIA system, starting with the Level 2 archive, we must have constant feedback on the many aspects and interconnections of the system as it is constructed. We need to display the data immediately in order for staff of the project to monitor the input, links, and calculations. And we need to provide for output to general users at the earliest possible stage, in order to accelerate the dissemination of global-level data, to draw more users and contributors into working with the system, and to begin contributing to public information and education as soon as possible. As the initial analysis and visualization will indicate, the work of assembling data in Mission 1 points in many directions and requires parallel work by a number of groups. As we turn to address Mission 2, many of these varying tasks will be drawn together to focus on reformulating the data collection into consistent materials that provide a global picture.

In this way, users will be able to experience the initial level of world-historical data exploration. This work is expected to have two advantages. On one hand, it is for getting the initial kinks out of the

DOI: 10.1057/9781137378972

programming for the expanded archive: assembly of data, construction of metadata, programming the search for data within the CHIA Archive, and conveying selected data for visualization. On the other hand, the initial visualization is to display a simplified version of world-historical data analysis, so that potential contributors of data and potential users of the resource will understand its potential more clearly.

## Spatio-temporal bridge

This application compares multiple datasets according to their spatial and temporal domains and for selected topical domains. It is a system for visualizing and analyzing datasets in the Level 1 Archive, surveying available datasets to match user-determined criteria. This application works for any dataset, whether fully digitized or not, for which the file-level metadata indicate the spatial domain (defined by point or polygon) and the temporal domain (in years for which data are included). That is, for contributors and users of the CHIA Level 1 archive who are not yet certain that they want to go through the Col*Fusion process of data integration, the Spatio-Temporal Bridge is an alternative and somewhat simpler system that compares datasets more than it integrates them. The application, developed by Kai Cao of the World History Center, portrays the selected files by spatial distribution (through the WorldMap application) and temporal distribution (in a newly produced time line). The user can focus at various scales of space and time, and see the number of files represented for each increment of time and space. Where files are very dense in number, the system is able to focus and distinguish them. In the main application, so far, the spatio-temporal data search has been applied to 526 social science dataverses (archives) in the Dataverse Network Archive, to report on the degree of density of existing studies, by space and time, for a given set of topics. The application, developed in association with Ben Lewis of the WorldMap project and Mercè Crosas of IQSS, has the potential to expand to spatial and statistical analysis.

One further device that should facilitate the sharing and publication of datasets is peer-reviewing, both for Level 1 and Level 2 datasets. That is, one begins by recognizing the integrity of each dataset, as prepared by its compiler. Published datasets represent immense efforts in compiling, editing, verifying, and documenting historical data. These data collections need to be recognized as contributions in themselves and should be granted such recognition in published statements by authorities in

DOI: 10.1057/9781137378972

the field. The *Journal of World-Historical Information*, a newly established academic journal associated with CHIA, is working to ensure that historical datasets are reviewed by qualified scholarly peers who confirm or question the assembly of the data and the value of the dataset for historical analysis.

# Notes

1    The House of Commons Parliamentary Papers have been digitized by Chadwyck-Healey and are searchable in their system. Extracting the data tables from these files and incorporating them into CHIA would take further arrangements: see http://parlipapers.chadwyck.com/home.do.
2    Project Tycho™: www.tycho.pitt.edu. See also Van Panhuis (2013, in press). This research was founded by the Bill and Melinda Gates Foundation and by the National Institutes of Health Modeling of Infectious Disease Agent (MIDAS) program.
3    Working on population data were Xi Zhang (Sociology) and Yongxu Huang (Public Health). Erin Jenkins (Public Health) worked on both climate and population data and wrote the project report.
4    See Chapter 6 for further discussion of the disease-climate-population project.
5    In addition, the World-Historical Dataverse website at Pitt also maintains an extensive list of online historical datasets, plus materials from research activities and presentations at Pitt (WHD).
6    As can be seen, this program of merging files through Col*Fusion is distinct from – if somewhat parallel to – the notion of 'linked data' (LinkedData). Col*Fusion is not a vision of linking the entire web file-level metadata, but is an infrastructure for integrating data within files.

DOI: 10.1057/9781137378972

# 5

# Mission 2: Creating a Comprehensive Historical Archive

Abstract: *This chapter centers on the two key steps prior to analyzing data at the global level: 'harmonizing' datasets to prepare them for linkage to one another and 'aggregation' to create files of steadily expanded scale, up to global levels in space, time, and topic. Objectives include creating comparable units in time and place, for instance by presenting big countries (Russia and China) in terms of regional subunits. Population, the most basic of human data, must be estimated for all regions. Harmonization requires consistent documentation – through algorithms developed by CHIA staff – by source, time, space, weights and measures, and uncertainty in observations. Particular effort goes into locating datasets for data-poor regions, to ensure that their metadata are included in the overall ontology. The data processed to this level are housed at Level 3 of CHIA's distributed archive.*

Keywords: aggregation; distributed archive; harmonization; metadata

Manning, Patrick. *Big Data in History*. Basingstoke: Palgrave Macmillan, 2013. DOI: 10.1057/9781137378972.

Step-by-step assembly of data is a necessary step along the road to creating a world-historical data resource. Only through these successive steps will we encounter the numerous problems that await us and develop the numerous innovations required for work at such a large scale. But if we move only at this incremental rate it will take forever for us to develop a serious world-historical data resource. This is shown in the slow pace at which social science researchers have moved in the process of consolidating local and national data into global data.

Historical data for various places and times have not been rendered compatible with one another, especially for Asia, Africa, and the Americas, and especially for times before the twentieth century. Even for the most obvious of commodities – wheat, rice, silver, cotton textiles, and iron – we do not have long-term, global statistical series on either production or commerce. It is true that a large body of historical data already exists, generally on the internet and more specifically in such repositories as the ICPSR and the Dataverse Network. Even these, however, are disaggregated sets of data with two very distinct levels of documentation – the high-level documentation of the repository system (SAS or SPSS statistical packages) and the documentation provided for constituent datasets by their creators. Most statistical data assembled by historical researchers, further, are held in Excel and other spreadsheet software, with no systematic documentation facilities. Thus, no magic bullet will turn existing repositories into globally analyzable bodies of data: existing data need essentially to be redocumented, and newly entered historical data need to be documented comprehensively. Such documentation requires both a consistent framework and the expertise of academic researchers – including those who constructed or transcribed the data and others with similar expertise. One of the benefits of using a crowdsourcing approach in gathering data is that it will cause all contributors of data to develop and work from a common schema of data definition. The difficulty, of course, will be in working out a consensus among historians and social scientists on that common schema.

Rather than wait for a gradual accretion of localized projects to bring about large-scale analysis, CHIA seeks to conduct a large-scale initiative to speed the transition into global social analysis. The data, technology, and readiness of researchers to collaborate are within reach. This collaborative has the experience and the organizational skills, and now seeks large-scale institutional support. CHIA can decisively address the remaining gap: it can advance global analysis in social sciences by leading

DOI: 10.1057/9781137378972

in creation of a consolidated system of information and also by resolving many attendant technical and organizational challenges. Whether CHIA remains the sole center for assembling global historical data and analysis or whether it attracts other major groupings so that CHIA becomes absorbed into a larger collaborative effort – the launching of this collaborative will speed and strengthen the long-overdue process of systematically documenting the human record.

Ultimately, a comprehensive world-historical archive requires data not only at the global level but also at the local level and at intermediate levels. In this way, the data will permit not only the identification of global dynamics but also the dynamics by which global and local patterns influence each other. For such analysis, electronic datasets present essential advantages over the previous system of print display. It is important that we break free of the limitations of conceptualizing data, especially tabular data, according to the long tradition of two-dimensional, printed tables. Print materials make it difficult to present data at various scales except by treating them as entirely separate issues. Print displays, when they indicate global totals, almost never show the local and regional constituents of the global totals; they do not facilitate a multi-scale analysis. Rapid computing and relational datasets, however, make it possible to look at all the levels at once – and thereby to develop the multi-dimensional view of data that is necessary for a consistently global perspective.

## A distributed global archive

CHIA's Mission 2 is to link and aggregate data from local levels up to the global level: the activities of this mission move files from Level 2 to Level 3 in the Archive. The CHIA Level 3 Archive is to be a comprehensive, global historical collection of consistent and connected data on human experience during the past several centuries. This Level 3 Archive will result from transformation, linkage, and aggregation of resources from the Level 2 Archive, where they have earlier been deposited by contributors. In administrative terms, it is most convenient for the data of the distributed global archive to be held within the CHIA Archive (with its three current repositories: the Pittsburgh Supercomputer Center, the CHIA server in Information Sciences at Pitt and the Dataverse Network). But exceptions to this approach are acceptable to CHIA – even large-scale

DOI: 10.1057/9781137378972

exceptions. That is, for data held by organizations that are willing to share data but need retain it in their own archives, it can be arranged for CHIA – when an analysis is to be conducted – to import the data via an API and wrapper, in a process parallel to the ingest of datasets in Level 1. The main potential problem of this approach – the possibility of undiscovered inconsistencies in the imported metadata – can be resolved with additional procedures. All in all, it should be possible to extend the CHIA Archive as needed, to support a continuously expanding documentation and analysis of historical human society.

Organization of data in the comprehensive archive requires that the documentation of space and time be at once systematic and flexible – that is, able to account for all the different ways that space and time are labeled in historical documents. In practical terms, the archive will begin with the systematic assembly of population data, and will go on to address a wide range of variables from the local to global levels. Accompanying this assembly of data is the work of data 'harmonization' – that is, the cleaning, fusion, integration, transformation, and aggregation of submitted datasets into larger and more comprehensive datasets. The archive will facilitate analysis of links among variables and among the various levels of social organization. In addition, the work of aggregating and linking data, since it brings further transformation of data, will also generate 'extended metadata' to record each of these modifications.

## 'Harmonizing' data for global analysis: extended metadata

'Harmonizing' is a term adopted here to refer to several different types of modification of raw data necessary to create a coherent, global dataset. The 'what, where, when, source' of the originally entered data are expected to have been documented at the previous level, through the Col*Fusion process. Here, additional transformations and aggregations will be required. Original submissions of data need to be cleaned of errors and integrated to resolve duplications and inconsistencies across datasets. Thereafter – along with the transformation of submitted data by language, geography, time, weights, measures and other criteria to make them compatible with other contributed datasets – comes the creation of 'extended metadata' to document further transformations. That is,

DOI: 10.1057/9781137378972

along with aggregation of data by scale (both geographic and temporal) in order to have consistent regional and global datasets created out the smaller datasets comes the creation of extended metadata to document the aggregation.[1] Once the Level 3 archive is fully developed, its volume of metadata will likely equal or exceed the volume of data.

To repeat a point made earlier, gathering a large number of datasets is not sufficient to produce global data – the data need to be merged into a comprehensive, relational data repository. Nor is it possible to create a comprehensive data repository through automated processing of the existing metadata – the terms of metadata are inconsistent with one another and, too often, major bits of information turn out simply to be missing. *Not only is it necessary to achieve consistency in the documentation of individual files but additional metadata must be created to account for harmonization and linkage of inconsistent local datasets and for aggregation to regional and global levels.*

Figure 5.1 provides a schematic summary of the full range of harmonization and aggregation processes conducted in Mission 2. Throughout these processes, each dataset maintains an attached set of metadata, updated steadily to account for each change in the dataset. At the stage of harmonization, each pair of datasets is rendered consistent with other datasets in the Level 3 archive according to numerous criteria. That is, harmonization procedures reconfirm the sources of each dataset, they adjust for the language in which each dataset was prepared, they check the identification of spaces associated with each dataset, they verify the time frame of each dataset (perhaps transforming from one calendar to another), they resolve any inconsistencies in weights and measures of variables, and they register each dataset according to its 'scale', the relative breadth of its time, space, and topical range. Further, the harmonization procedures check for instances of multiple observations on given variables, and apply algorithms to select the best of the competing observations. For all of the elements of each dataset, the harmonization procedures assess and record the level of uncertainty in the various observations (Zadorozhny et al. 2008).

In harmonizing spatial data, Mission 2 is to apply a world-historical gazetteer. A world-historical gazetteer is more than a list of locations and descriptions of those locations. The gazetteer must account for several types of locations (including physical features, administrative units, and the 'places' or toponyms of ordinary human usage), for changes over time in the character of each place, and for varying degrees of specificity

DOI: 10.1057/9781137378972

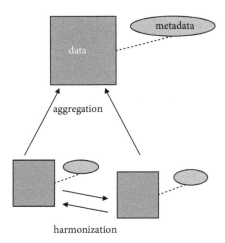

FIGURE 5.1    *Mission 2: harmonizing and aggregating data*

in describing each place (from places fully mapped in geospatial terms to places for which we have a name and little more). Are spatial references nested within each other – as for cities within provinces? How does one account for shifts in boundaries or shifts in names? The full development of a world-historical gazetteer requires resolution of these conceptual issues plus systematic incorporation of worldwide data on places: the gazetteer may be distributed among several repositories, thus enabling it to handle special cases and exceptions to general patterns.

One major project, underway as of this writing, addresses the construction of a world-historical gazetteer. The Pelagios 3 project is generating content for the world before 1492 to go into three related gazetteers: those of Pleiades (Center for Study of the Ancient World at New York University), China Historical GIS (Center for Geographic Analysis at Harvard), and PastPlace (University of Portsmouth).[2] The project includes an interoperability model so that a single query can address all three gazetteers. A second project, proposed by CHIA, would organize a 2014 conference, assembling participants from all major groups working in gazetteer development, to set common criteria for a world-historical gazetteer. Especially because CHIA seeks to develop and estimate data for all areas of the world during the last four centuries, including those not currently documented, there is a need for maximum clarity on how to conduct spatial documentation on poorly documented regions in the context of a global dataset that also includes fully detailed spatial data

DOI: 10.1057/9781137378972

on well-documented regions. These two projects indicate that many of the best minds are working with increasing cooperation, developing the format and the details for recording geographic data globally: their discussions should open up the additional steps that need to be taken. Successful resolution of these spatial issues will advance the quality and interoperability of historical datasets generally and, specifically for CHIA, will provide the basis for a spatial search engine to work effectively within the CHIA Archive.

Similarly, the classification of time must be worked out in comprehensive detail. If time frames such as years, months, and decades seem relatively unproblematic, they nevertheless contain potential inconsistencies. Calendars are inconsistent over time and space. The Gregorian calendar, now in near universal use during the twenty-first century, was not at all in universal use before the third millennium.[3] To locate an event or process within a 'year' may refer to a closed unit of 365 days or may refer to an open-ended subunit within that year. Decades are clearly ten years in length, but they are accounted in some situations as beginning with a year '0' (e.g., 1840), and in other situations as beginning with a year '1' (e.g., 1881). Temporal references can also be vague: 'before 1800', 'during the late seventeenth century'. In chronologies or data series there may be gaps, so that to have data 'from 1740 to 1880' does not necessarily mean complete documentation within those limits. The temporal classification system needs to account for the varying levels of specificity in temporal records, and create a system maximizing the possibility of linking and comparing various records to each other by coming up with appropriate parallels in identifying their time frame.

The classification of topics is the most wide-ranging and eclectic dimension of documenting data. For twentieth-century commerce and for museum holdings, substantial efforts have gone into developing classifications especially for material goods, and the process of documentation within CHIA will draw upon these systems (CIDOC). But the overall system of documentation within CHIA will have to link and accommodate not only the description of material goods but also social relations, governmental structures, health, and climate. The documentation of population data, among the most basic and pervasive categories of data to be considered, exemplifies the complications. Populations are sometimes given as numeric totals, and at other times they are broken down by age and sex. While distinction by sex is relatively straightforward, estimates of precise age are notoriously inconsistent

DOI: 10.1057/9781137378972

and age groups have been defined in so many different ways that it is difficult to prepare consistent summaries. Nevertheless, it is important to develop clear summaries and breakdowns of population data, as they provide important links among the various social science theories.

In addition to the revision of data and metadata in individual files, there will arise problems of contradictions or inconsistencies in data across files. That is, multiple files may have overlapping or inconsistent data on certain variables. The time frames or topical content attributed to variables may overlap. In such cases, it is necessary to develop procedures on whether to include one, another, or all candidates for the values of the variable in question. This question will come up particularly in the case of documents for which topics are close substitutes for one another, such as closely related types of textiles, or for diseases that are not diagnosed with great specificity. For such inconsistencies in data, Vladimir Zadorozhny has developed algorithms that are helpful in determining conditions in which one or another solution is shown to be most probably the best (Zadorozhny et al. 2008, Zadorozhny et al. 2013).

The issue of uncertainty in the values attributed to variables, as always, remains a prime concern in harmonizing data. Harmonization will both expand and reduce uncertainty, through various processes. The correction of errors and inconsistencies in time, place, and in topical dimensions reduces uncertainty significantly for certain variables, but the conduct of additional calculations in making transformations adds marginally to the uncertainty of the full range of variables.

The maintenance of this huge amount of metadata will be laborious and expensive, but the effort will be worth the cost. Surely the biggest benefit of preserving all of the metadata is that it ensures that the dataset can be reproduced. That is, it should be possible to reproduce the full archive, on the fly, from the Base Archive by replicating all the calculations. Similarly, if it is learned that some of the calculations need to be carried out in different form, it is possible to establish the full range of implications of the new calculations, throughout the archive. For instance, imagine that one learns that a price index – used widely throughout the archive to deflate value statistics from current to constant value – has been found to be in error or has been superseded by an improved price index. In that case, case corrections would have to be made throughout and additional metadata would need to be recorded. With fully upgraded metadata, based on strong standards, it will be possible to recalculate each value precisely, on the fly, thus preserving

DOI: 10.1057/9781137378972

the value of the repository and its elements over time.[4] The alternative is that whole datasets might have to be abandoned and recreated from the beginning. In particular, many of the global indices created and widely circulated to describe national statistics for the past 50 years appear to contain data but no substantial metadata, so that if price indices or commercial volumes were to be recalculated, there would be no available basis for recalculation: the choice would be to use outdated figures or simply junk the dataset.

## Aggregating data files

The remaining work of Mission 2 is aggregation of datasets. The purpose of aggregating files at one scale is to create data at an expanded scale. One process by which files will be aggregated within CHIA is that users will submit queries that link existing datasets: the resulting linked datasets, in addition to undergoing analysis by the users, will be retained and archived for future reference. More systematically, CHIA staff will be able to construct aggregated files out of existing files, for instance to ensure that the archive includes continental and hemispheric totals for relevant variables. While aggregation by space and time will be the starting point for such work, the more complex task is how to aggregate by topic. This will require fuller development of a topical ontology, in which we will see whether commodities, services, social processes, and even cultural issues can be divided into coherent and nested categories, or whether overlaps in categories will remain significant. In each case, such processes of aggregation will bring about the creation of extended metadata – including reliability measures – so that the resulting files will be fully documented. Meanwhile, discussion continues within the CHIA project about the relative benefits of constructing aggregate files as a separate stage, as described above, as contrasted with relying on queries to construct aggregate files by improvisation and on the fly, assuming that we will have access to high computing capacity and to the full range of datasets in the distributed archive.

Further, the CHIA project will seek ways to link its efforts with other large data-collection projects, notably CLIO-INFRA (economic historians based in the Netherlands) and Terra Populus (census and environmental analysis based at the University of Minnesota). These connections will expand the global collection of data to include population in the post-1950 period and economic historical data worldwide.

DOI: 10.1057/9781137378972

The processes of harmonization and aggregation will create new data. This system of global historical data, once initially developed, will be able to expand with the location of additional data or inclusion of additional collaborators. In particular, to anticipate the quantity of historical data likely to be included in the Level 3 Archive, it is important to become clear about the difference between *existing data* and *new data* in history. This can be explained by comparison with Big Data in the natural sciences: while one part of this project is the collection and digitization of known historical records, another part of it will result in the discovery and creation of immense amounts of *new* historical data. As in geology and astronomy, even though the facts of the past remain unchanged, today's developments of theories and techniques will result in the development of huge amounts of empirical information on the past: for instance, estimates of past levels of temperature and precipitation that were not previously known. Similarly, historical research will develop previously unknown data on population, levels of commerce, and patterns of inequality. Through inclusion, aggregation, and documentation of the full amount of such data, the Level 3 Archive will expand to the petabyte level.

# Notes

1   Within the general category of 'harmonization', 'cleaning' refers to correcting errors in individual data values, 'fusion' refers to consolidating overlapping or duplicate data, 'transformation' refers to standardization of weights and measures as well as language translation, and 'aggregation' refers to consolidating files to develop data files into files of larger scale in space, time, and topic. Work of constructing the archive will further clarify the details and overlaps of these processes.

2   The Pelagios 3 project is supported by the Andrew W. Mellon Foundation.

3   Nations that still give official recognition to calendars other than the Gregorian calendar include Iran, Afghanistan, Ethiopia, Saudi Arabia, Israel, India, Bangla Desh, Japan, and Thailand.

4   One challenging but important issue is that of finding ways to record metadata so that they are linked to each observation within the data resource. Once this is achieved, it will be possible to make corrections and updates throughout the Archive, on the fly.

DOI: 10.1057/9781137378972

# 6

## Mission 3: Analyzing and Visualizing Data Worldwide

**Abstract:** *A global historical archive, once created, must be analyzed appropriately. One side of such analysis requires specific techniques of computation and representation to implement analyses. Another side of it requires an appropriate conceptualization of society at the global level, sound application of social science theory, and alternation among multiple perspectives. In two important feedback loops, data-mining will rely on computational systems to seek out unrecognized relations within the Archive, and systems of analysis will estimate and simulate missing data. In each case the results of these exercises will be incorporated into the Archive. Visualization, beginning with geographic visualization of global data, will expand to temporal and topical visualization at various scales, and more generally to visualization of information, concept, strategy, and metaphor. CHIA is to be open to high-level analysis by researchers but also to more basic questions from teachers and students. Results of user queries and interpretations will be added to the archive; feedback from analysis of the data will bring modification to the work of Mission 1 and Mission 2.*

**Keywords:** computation; missing data; representation; social science data; visualization

Manning, Patrick. *Big Data in History*. Basingstoke: Palgrave Macmillan, 2013. DOI: 10.1057/9781137378972.

The overall problem in Mission 3 is how to interpret data up to the global level. It is to take the data prepared up to Level 3 of the archive and to analyze, mine, and visualize it; results of this interpretation are then held in Level 4 and Level 5 of the archive. While analysis is commonly thought of as the last step of work with a dataset, here visualization and analysis of data will take place at every stage of CHIA's work. Thus, at the initial stage of CHIA we set up the Spatio-Temporal Bridge to visualize the distribution of datasets in time and space and thereby assist in selecting datasets for inclusion in the Archive so as to achieve an appropriate density of data in time and space. This and later versions of tools for analysis and visualization will provide feedback and ensure that the needs of users remain central to the design and construction of the system as the data are moved from level to level of the archive. Visualization of the data, while it begins with elementary summaries of variables and their descriptive data, must also represent clearly the multiple forms of interactions among variables. Data visualization must go far beyond spreadsheets: it must draw upon the sophisticated, multi-dimensional representation of variables that have been developed in studies of climate, genomics, and other areas of the natural sciences.

Figure 6.1 indicates the steps of visualization and analysis. One may first imagine the user as a CHIA staff person building the Archive. In this case the user selects files for analysis from the Level 4 archive, where each file remains accompanied by its metadata. The analysis takes the form of a query submitted to the Archive, and the results are returned to the user as output. These processes of analysis build the Archive in two ways: they conduct estimation of missing data to expand the empirical content of the Archive and they implement data-mining to locate unsuspected relationships within the Archive. In some cases these will be expanded analyses of known relationships – as between climate variation and agricultural output; in addition, techniques of data mining may permit identification of relations and patterns far beyond those now known. The results of this CHIA staff analysis provide updates to the Level 4 Archive. If the user is a researcher, the process is quite parallel: the user selects criteria for retrieval of data from the Level 4 Archive, submits queries that include the requested steps in analysis, and obtains a return of the output. The next step, Level 5, is the display or visualization of the output: the user selects the form of visualization from the available options, and of course the user develops the interpretation of results from the combination of the reported data and the user's perspective.

DOI: 10.1057/9781137378972

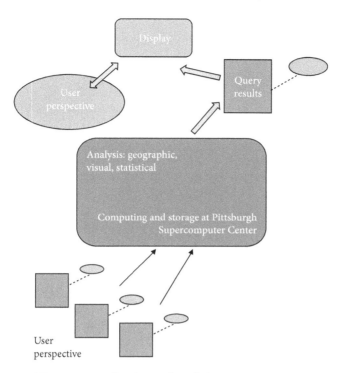

**FIGURE 6.1**   *Mission 3: visualization and analysis*

## Global conceptualization

The effort to identify and represent global patterns is made more difficult by the long-established philosophy of scientific analysis. Positivistic philosophy, gradually perfected in the scientific work of the nineteenth century, focused on breaking big problems into small problems, developing solutions to the small problems, and extending those results to the understanding of larger issues. (Darwin's mechanism of natural selection in biological evolution and Alfred Marshall's price theory in economics stand out as examples.) To this day, the tendency to analyze by breaking big problems into small problems remains preeminent. Thus a search on Google goes from the general to the specific and a search on Wikipedia leads progressively on a tree out to the leaves of the most specific aspects of each topic. The problem of global analysis does not reject this focus on specificity, but it requires that it be balanced

DOI: 10.1057/9781137378972

with a focus on the global and encompassing nature of systems. If a Google search progressively narrows the investigation, can there be a search system that progressively broadens the scope in an orderly way? Will we have access to search systems that explore issues at multiple scales? As we explore the dynamics of historical change, will we have tools to facilitate shifting the temporal frame and the spatial frame of those dynamics? An example from the field of genomics shows how analysis at multiple scales is ultimately necessary for scientific advance: after the initial discovery of the double-helix structure of DNA molecules, attention focused for more than a generation on the specific sequences of amino acids within DNA, in order to know which RNA and protein molecules were produced by each sequence – this was the *nature* of each gene. Ultimately, however, it became clear that processes at a broader scale were also essential to genetic reproduction: the overall folding and shape of the DNA molecules – and of proteins fit next to them – determined the *expression* of genes, the circumstances in which genetic reproduction would actually take place. It should not be surprising to find analogies in human affairs, in which some elements of a key social process take place at a localized level while others take place at a broader level.

## Rich data, poor data: theory and worldwide documentation

The typical approach to collecting historical data has been to find the best and most complete existing collections of data and work with them. Sometimes it is the case that these are the most important data as well as being the most available. But otherwise this may not be the case. For instance, the most readily available migration data – focusing on Europeans crossing the North Atlantic – long made it appear that these Europeans were the most migratory of humans. Just over a decade ago, however, a systematic look at Asian data showed that migration from China and India each roughly equaled that from all of Europe, for the period 1850–1940 (McKeown 2006).

In order to develop comprehensive world-historical data, it is necessary to gather data on all the regions, all the populations, and all the time periods. As a result, researchers will need to devote extra

DOI: 10.1057/9781137378972

effort to regions and time periods for which data are in short supply. That certainly means that CHIA researchers will need to concentrate on regions such as Africa, Southeast Asia, Central Asia, and Latin America, inviting scholars in those regions to affiliate with CHIA.[1] Data collection in data-poor regions will require intensive application of established techniques and development of new techniques. That is, archival and family-held data, in numerous languages, will need to be located and digitized. Scattered publications will need to be located, relevant data identified, and then digitized. When direct data are not available – as on population, trade, or politics – researchers will have to work to develop indirect estimates. So work with data-poor domains will require advanced techniques for estimation and simulation of missing data. For instance, current work is relying on techniques of simulation to prepare decennial estimates of African population from 1650 to 1950, including numerous regions within Africa (Manning and Nickleach, forthcoming). In ways such as this, the study of data-poor regions can advance the CHIA project overall: development of techniques for estimating missing data will clarify theoretical relationships among social science variables, and the resulting advances in estimation and cross-disciplinary theory can then by applied to data-rich domains as well.

In expanding work on historical domains where data are in relatively short supply and of relatively poor quality, social scientists can learn from the work of natural scientists, whose search for data has led them to work closely with research institutions around the world. Especially in the fields of astronomy, climatology, and the various fields of biology, researchers work increasingly through collaborations with universities, research institutes, and individual scholars from all over the world.[2] Another way that social scientists can learn from the advances of natural sciences is to look for a sharpening of the distinction between *existing data* and *new data* in history. *Existing data*, recorded in historical documents, have simply to be digitized and transferred into CHIA. *New data*, which are somewhat analogous to experimental data in the natural sciences, are located through simulation and other forms of study of the relationships among known data. Thus, while one part of the CHIA project is the collection and digitization of known historical records, another part of it will result in the discovery and creation of immense amounts of *new* historical data.[3]

DOI: 10.1057/9781137378972

Population data will be developed as the basic core of data for the global data resource. Population is included, in one way or another, in all social science theory and data collections. The establishment of a relatively universal dataset on human population for the past several centuries – with attention to regional breakdown, composition by age and sex, and other available demographic data – will provide the empirical grounding for the global dataset, to which other data will be gradually added. In addition, the work of building the global population dataset will help clarify the handling of population data in various aspects of social science theory. Feedback within these processes of analysis will help to improve the quality of regional and global population data, including changes over time.

Analysis in the social sciences has developed impressively in the last 50 years, with many advances at micro-, macro-, and (increasingly) meso-levels of theory and research. Most of these advances, however, have been specific and local, making the social sciences increasingly diversified and subdivided. Far less attention has gone into linking the sub-theories of each discipline to each other. For instance, behavioral approaches have become influential in microeconomics, but it is not yet clear whether the behavioral approach has implications for macroeconomic analysis (Etzioni 2011). Sociological studies at micro and macro levels diverge considerably from each other; studies in comparative politics focus on national government almost to the exclusion of trends and traditions in local governance (Calhoun and Duster 2005). In addition, general reviews of social sciences tend to compare their parallel silos rather than focus on their interactions or on overall developments in the logic, philosophy, and empirical base of social science knowledge. In particular, the increasingly acute problems of social inequality have not yet led to large-scale, cross-disciplinary efforts to address the interacting dimensions of inequality in economic, social, political, and cultural affairs.

The social sciences have thus responded to globalization more with intensive development of sub-theories than with extensive explorations across disciplinary frontiers. For all their sophistication, they give minimal attention to change over time, global patterns, and cross-disciplinary effects.[4] All in all, the current state of social science analysis accords low priority to studies that are long-term in their time frame, multi-scale or global in their spatial scope, and cross-disciplinary in their analysis of social dynamics. Yet the current problems of globalization suggest that there is a great need for information at all of these scales, despite their

DOI: 10.1057/9781137378972

relative complexity. Investing in the creation of global data will launch this wide range of discussions.

I offer a personal example of how theory and simulation, in interaction with available empirical data, can develop useful estimates of missing data. Thus, the population of the African continent, roughly one-sixth or one-seventh of the human total, is not documented with detailed censuses before 1950, and is known only by speculative estimates for the early twentieth and late nineteenth century. Yet we have shreds of evidence. In a few cases, we have estimates of levels of fertility and mortality of African populations; we have more detailed estimates for these variables in other parts of the tropical world at the same time. We have quite detailed information, retrieved in a great campaign of collaborative and competitive research from 1970 to 2000, on the size and composition of the Atlantic slave trade. We have less specific but still substantial estimates of slave exports across the Indian Ocean, the Red Sea, and the Sahara. Further, it is possible to make estimates of the number of people enslaved in the great nineteenth-century expansion of enslavement within Africa – and, by extension, the excess mortality in sub-Saharan Africa during that time. At each stage, this work can identify the error margin or uncertainty in each figure. Assembling all of these empirical data, demographic assumptions, and empirical data, it is possible to estimate African population (by total size, age, and sex composition) (Manning 1990; Manning 2010; Manning and Nickleach forthcoming). My overall estimates of African population, using this collection of methods, work back from a 1950 total of 320 million to a 1900 continental total of 140 million, and to a 1700 population that was also 140 million. These estimates include regional sub-totals, plus estimates of migrants to receiving zones in the Americas, North Africa, the Middle East, and the Indian Ocean. Such estimates can be tested against other data on African regions in the eighteenth and nineteenth century, leading perhaps to revision of population figures and perhaps to development of additional estimates for other dimensions of African society.

# Analysis and data-mining

The combined  tasks of analyzing data at the worldwide level requires overall clarity, access to detail, and the identification of unexpected

DOI: 10.1057/9781137378972

patterns. 'Analysis' typically means quantitative and statistical analysis of dependent variables as they are influenced by independent variables. Linear regression (the least-squares model) is a common technique for seeking out cause-and-effect relationships among variables: it is applicable for cases where most of the variables are interval variables, though it allows for incorporation of some nominal and ordinal variables. Typically such analyses have been done among variables within the domain of economics or politics. Analysis within CHIA will begin at this established level of social science analysis, but it is sure to extend to several other types of analysis, including analysis of textual and visual records.

Within the CHIA project, there is an effort to locate relationships among variables somewhat further afield. To illustrate how the CHIA project has begun to address these big issues, here is a further discussion of the initial work on linking disease, climate, and population data for twentieth-century U.S.[5] While the total amounts of data in each category were huge, data had to be cut back for early-stage exploration. Locations were cut down to cities of the eastern United States seaboard; out of diseases, measles and polio were selected; climate data were cut back to daily average temperature; and population data for the selected cities were recorded (by age and sex) for census years. Immediately there arose the discrepancy in time frame of the data: climate data were daily, disease data were weekly, and population data were decennial. Even after the laborious work of locating or calculating annual census totals, there remained few observations on population. The analysis did confirm the seasonal character of measles (with most cases in the spring) and polio (with most cases in the fall). This example may help to convey both the potential and the complexity of analysis and visualization at the global level. Climatological research has clarified global patterns – the primacy of the power of solar glare on lands of the northern hemisphere in generating the patterns of global climate – but it has also documented the specificity of local climates within the overall global pattern. Visual representations, however, have yet to become fully convincing in balancing the global and local patterns of climate.

The archive will also be subjected to systematic data-mining. Data-mining is a system for exploring and extracting unsuspected relationships: previously unknown but interesting patterns such as groups of data records (cluster analysis), unusual records (anomaly detection) and dependencies (association rule mining). This involves analysis without

DOI: 10.1057/9781137378972

hypothesis, usually involving use of such database techniques as spatial indices. These computational techniques conduct eclectic explorations of all possible relationships among data within the resource, and report instances where correlations arise. Once the CHIA resource becomes sufficiently large in the volume of its data, it will be time to try out data-mining techniques.

Each step in analysis (including data-mining and the estimation of missing data) involves submission of queries to domains within the Archive; after analysis, the system returns detailed responses to the user. These responses will be preserved, incorporated into the Archive, and will become part of the basis for later interpretation. At least conceptually and perhaps in practice, the elements of the CHIA Archive from Level 1 to Level 5 will be held within a single resource: CHIA is carrying out initial work to that end with the Pittsburgh Supercomputing Center. At the most basic level (Level 1), this comprehensive archive will hold the datasets submitted by individual and institutional contributors, so that users may consult and cite the data at that level. At the next level of integration (Level 2), the archive will hold revised datasets that have undergone cleaning, various types of harmonization, and are described in terms of the uniform CHIA system of documentation – including both 'basic metadata' for each dataset and 'extended metadata' to account for transformation and harmonization of datasets to make them mutually consistent. At still another level of integration (Level 3), the archive will hold aggregated datasets in which the harmonized but localized datasets are assembled into regional and global datasets over short or long periods of time – plus the additional metadata to describe the aggregation process. Further, Levels 4 and 5 of the archive include the results of analysis and advanced visualization, as they expand the relationships known to exist among the data. The volume of data in this comprehensive archive will reach the petabyte level.

# Visualization

One of the great successes in global visualization has been the 'Gapminder' framework as developed by Hans Rosling. In his lively presentations at annual TED meetings, Rosling was able to display surprising changes in global social and economic development (TED; *GAPMINDER*). His approach provides an important example of the type

DOI: 10.1057/9781137378972

of display of variables and pairs of variables that the CHIA Archive will provide to researchers, teachers, and students. In addition to this step forward, however, many more advances are required in the visualization and analysis of global data. For instance, Gapminder is limited to a comparison of national units for the one or two centuries during which those units have existed. At base, it includes just two dimensions, although clever handling of colors and bubbles enables the inclusion of additional variables. Gapminder does not display multiple levels of aggregation, from local to global, and its display of time is limited to one-year cross-sections. In sum, the display of world-historical data must go beyond cross-sectional national comparisons to include multiple levels, varying spatial aggregations, and exploration of change over varying temporal sequences.[6]

Spatial units, for instance, cannot reasonably be restricted to those of modern nations for this historical dataset. For proper comparison over time, the huge national units of Russia, China, the United States, India, and Brazil need to be analyzed in terms of smaller units, comparable in size to European or African countries. The CHIA project will thus attempt to identify relevant and persistent subunits for each of the large national units among them as well as for the nation as a whole. Yet any attempt to trace such units over four centuries encounters the shifting political and imperial boundaries as well as great changes in population density.

There exist analogous problems in visualizing analysis over time. The exploration of global patterns over time must take place not only through year-by-year chronology, but also through longer periods (to address cycles in economy and climate) and shorter periods (to assess seasonal variation). Time must be considered not only in absolute, chronological terms, but also in relative terms, to account for the life cycle of individuals and the creation and maturation of economic and social institutions.

More generally the system of visualization must reach as far as our conceptualization. For instance, it must address both aggregated and disaggregated variables: we want to know not only about changes in the level of wheat production and trade over time, but also about changes in the total caloric intake of humans over time. Different types of data will lead to different emphases in visualization. Thus, climatic data will bring an emphasis on the theories that play such a role in climatic modeling, while genetic data will bring a focus on the diseases that provide important genetic markers. In addition, general studies of visualization

DOI: 10.1057/9781137378972

allow for visualization of information, concept, strategy, metaphor, and combinations of these (PTVM).

## CHIA for researchers and teachers

The approach of CHIA requires that its resources be available to general users – especially researchers and teachers – as soon as possible. As a result, it is clear that CHIA plans for analysis and visualization and must prepare for three main types of users: CHIA project staff seeking feedback on how to improve aspects of the program; researchers seeking sophisticated results on world-historical patterns; teachers seeking basic results on global patterns that can inform and inspire their students. Since earlier sections of this book have emphasized project development and advanced research, this section emphasizes the ways that CHIA can serve the interests of teachers and students.

Because conceptualizing the world first presents itself as a geographical issue, teachers may well choose to begin by exploring data to compare and link regions of the world. The organization of materials in the CHIA resource will make it possible to alternate among regional, national, and continental views of the world. Next, since the focus of human society is on people, teachers and students may wish to emphasize population: total populations by region, but also breakdowns by age and sex, by birth and death rates, and by migration. Students could then look at weather patterns, past and present, for various areas of the world, and link weather to other factors. If the contents of the CHIA resource can be documented in sufficiently clear terms, it will be possible for teachers and students to ask how government has worked and changed around the world, at levels from the locality to the empire. Students will also be able to trace the occasional breakdown of government in war and conflict. They will be able to compare the changing types of work over time and space and get a sense of how families have changed in their size, activities, and how they bring up their children. Naturally there will be plenty of evidence on major products in agriculture, handicrafts, and industry – on their quantities, trade, production, and changing design. With time, CHIA will be able to add to its archive such cultural information as details on languages, cultural practices, education, and literacy. Students will have an opportunity to explore as far as they want, and will also get practice in making choices as they face an overload of information.

DOI: 10.1057/9781137378972

Users will be able to comment on data and to correct it as appropriate. Teachers will be able to download units from the archive, selecting and analyzing according to their wishes. Yet the problem of having teachers download units from the archive is that of intellectual property: how will it be possible to maintain recognition of the source archives, the historians and the developers whose work underlies the data? How will it be possible to convey to students a sense that the data are not just abstract, true facts but statements resulting from the work and collaboration of a stream of workers? CHIA's visualization applications will have to make clear that output data do not exist by themselves – that the information on sources and transformations are an indissoluble part of every element of output data. This will not be an easy standard to maintain in a world where many users will be seeking quick and definitive answers, yet CHIA should be able to present its output in such a fashion as to encourage an ongoing discussion about sources and methods among the users.

In parallel with steady improvement and expansion of its system of data collection, documentation, archiving, and analysis, the CHIA group expects also to reach out to other groups of researchers, in various disciplines, who have been developing large-scale data resources. One such outstanding group is CLIO-INFRA, composed of leading scholars in economic and social history, based at the International Institute for Social History in Amsterdam (CLIO-INFRA). Like CHIA, CLIO-INFRA is a collaboration of institutions: Groningen Growth and Development Centre, International Institute of Social History, Utrecht University, and the Data Archiving and Networked Services (The Hague). CLIO-INFRA has set up 'data hubs' to work on collection of specific sorts of economic-historical data, focusing for instance on human capital, population, and standard of living; the group works closely with other economic historians who have developed historical data on wages and prices.

A second collaborative group works primarily on population data, especially censuses by national governments, and links of population with environmental data. This group – Terra Populus – based at the Minnesota Population Center has recently gained support for creating a consolidated digital data resource out of government censuses of nations throughout the world, focusing on the period since 1960 (Terra Populus). This project represents a major step forward in global data resources, notably in population data. It relies significantly on the work of the United Nations Office of Population, which has worked diligently to clarify and improve the quality of census returns and population

DOI: 10.1057/9781137378972

estimates for countries throughout the world, but especially for recently decolonized nations (UNPOP). Most of the data are already in digital form, though the Terra Populus group still faces the serious task of making the various datasets sufficiently consistent to be able to aggregate them across national lines. Similarly, there is the question of whether to make sub-national population data available, especially for large and populous countries. For CHIA, meanwhile, work with groups such as CLIO-INFRA and Terra Populus holds forth the promise of adding substantial economic and demographic data to a collaborative archive, which would form the core data of a universal historical data resource.

## Notes

1  I met in August 2013 with Pablo Gentili, Executive Secretary of CLACSO, and also with Ebrima Sall, Executive Secretary of CODESRIA (CLACSO, CODESRIA). For the case of CLACSO, the secretariat will facilitate establishment of links between its participating research groups and CHIA. For the case of CODESRIA, the central office will host a description of the CHIA project and its website will host a version of the CHIA Archive focusing on African data.

2  A striking example is the process of discovering the El Niño Southern Oscillation, where discoveries in early and mid-twentieth century led to a rapid accumulation of knowledge at the end of the century (Cushman 2003).

3  For instance, historians' work in piecing together of evidence from merchant correspondence is leading to evidence on commercial networks, both overland and maritime, that linked the early modern world. These networks, not previously known but of great historical significance, correspond to new historical data. For several good examples of this research, see the chapters in Mukherjee 2011.

4  Sociology and anthropology have little close contact, development economics has little to do with economic history, and the links of demography and health are only now coming under serious study.

5  See Chapter 4 for the introduction to this project.

6  The discussion to follow, on the types of analysis to be conducted, builds upon the initial list of analyses provided in Chapter 2.

DOI: 10.1057/9781137378972

# 7
# Comparisons: Big Data across Time and Disciplines

Abstract: *Just as knowledge of the past is important to current policy, so also is past practice in data collection important to guiding the work of CHIA. This chapter reviews the past 70 years of work in developing social science datasets, and also the parallel development of modeling in climate and genetics. The narratives of creation of archives and analyses on climate and genetics show the interplay of theory, historical data, technology, and changing public concerns, which led in each case to important advances in knowledge. It is argued that parallel steps and equivalent success can reasonably be expected in creation of a world historical archive.*

Keywords: climatology; genetics; history

Manning, Patrick. *Big Data in History*. Basingstoke: Palgrave Macmillan, 2013. DOI: 10.1057/9781137378972.

DOI: 10.1057/9781137378972

The majority of this book has focused on the technical problems of constructing a world-historical resource, making the argument that the project, while complex and expensive, is feasible and highly valuable. In this chapter we draw back from the specifics of the CHIA project. More broadly, we consider what steps have already been taken toward creating and archiving global historical data, what obstacles lie in the way of such work, and what parallel experiences with global archives might exist in fields outside of human history. The chapter traces the development of social science datasets from 1945 forward, then concisely narrates the creation of global historical archives for climate and the human genome, arguing that those experiences provide numerous parallels and useful lessons for CHIA. The chapter concludes with a discussion of how the global historical archive ought to be structured and where it might best be housed.

The era since World War II has brought accelerating efforts to collect social science data on national levels and growing efforts in comparison of national data. Looking back from the present, we can conceptualize these earlier programs as prototypical campaigns in global studies. The catastrophes of worldwide war, ending with the explosion of atomic devices in two major cities, provoked widespread reflection on global patterns and on the direction of human society overall. As the United Nations Organization formed in San Francisco in late 1945, it adopted a charter including UNESCO, the United Nations Educational, Social, and Cultural Organization – an organization to facilitate international scientific collaboration in all fields, in addition to its missions in education and culture. UNESCO appointed its first Director-general in 1946: in British-born biologist Julian Huxley, UNESCO found an energetic and visionary leader who laid out plans for collaboration on a scale that seemed headed toward compensating for the relentless national competition and enmity that had brought such devastating warfare. Huxley articulated the scientific philosophy of UNESCO as 'a scientific world humanism, global in extent and evolutionary in background' (Huxley 1946:6). Yet within UNESCO, Huxley expected social sciences to work not really at a universal level, but through comparison of cultural or national groups.

The social sciences worked within those cultural and political boundaries for the following half-century; within those limits, nevertheless, remarkable advances in scope and method were achieved. The area-studies movement brought substantial expansion of study on Asia, Africa, and Latin America, encouraging comparative analysis of national and local subunits. Macroeconomics arose as an important new field;

DOI: 10.1057/9781137378972

social and economic history developed productive quantitative methods; and spreadsheets brought a quantum leap in applications of demography (Preston et al. 2000). Meanwhile, that same post-war era brought massive globalization – in which global literacy and health advanced impressively, while political constellations changed repeatedly. In that context it is remarkable how little the social sciences have done to adopt a new mission of developing coordinated study of human society. One still awaits the big advances in linking information and analysis across disciplines, time, and space. The CHIA project can facilitate the next step, linking the disciplines and linking historical and contemporary studies within them.

In the natural sciences, since the formation of UNESCO, well-funded systems have developed impressive institutions, supporting research that unified analysis from micro-level to universal scales: examples include CERN in physics, the U.S. National Center for Biotechnology, and the Long Term Ecological Research Network. These institutions facilitated advances in research, at once responding to and creating the current explosion in scientific information (Bowker 2008). Where was the equivalent higher-order study in the social sciences? The explosion in social science information is arguably just as rapid, not only through creation of new and contemporary data but also through growing access to historical data brought by new techniques. The historical data include advances in health, earth science, and genomics with social scientific implications. Nonetheless, social scientists are only now expressing expanded interest in global issues and therefore in global data. The brief review to follow explores the traditions and antecedents on which social scientists will draw in creating global data.

## Social sciences from the 1940s

An overview of the period since World War II reveals three stages or generations of global analysis in social sciences. The first generation of global studies opened in the 1940s with post-war advances in conceptualization; the second generation opened in the 1980s with new computational techniques and perceptions of contemporary globalization; and the third generation of global studies is opening now with advances in historical and cross-disciplinary depth. At the initial stage, the formation of UNESCO was part of a post-war boom in enthusiasm that included what may be called the first generation of global studies – a

DOI: 10.1057/9781137378972

policy-oriented, eclectic, short-term set of concerns led by attention to 'modernization' and focusing on political, economic, and sometimes ecological issues. These early days of global studies centered on analysis of international relations in the early Cold War era, when atomic war was a daily threat. This era of disciplinary splintering was complemented by the rise of encompassing trends in social science analysis. Concerns about population growth and the emergence of ecological movements brought expansion of global study to further disciplines (Manning 2003). The first generation of research in global studies created a number of major institutions and important databases (HRAF, ICPSR, NBER, OECD, WB). For economic historical data over the long run, B. R. Mitchell began his monumental individual statistical compilation with European historical statistics, and gradually expanded both his geographic and temporal scope (Mitchell 2003). These studies were overwhelmingly national though sometimes imperial in scope.

Technology in the first generation of global studies relied initially on manual compilations but changed sharply with the expansion in social statistics and early computers. The post-war quantitative studies in politics, economics, sociology, and history, however, focused on small datasets and on community-level or at most national-level scope (Fogel and Engerman 1974). An important if marginal exception was the international literature on the volume and direction of the Atlantic slave trade (Manning 1996). In conceptual terms, the first generation of global studies, the era of worldwide decolonization, brought great advances in global scholarly thinking at the practical level, in that the dramatic expansion of area-studies scholarship brought a more inclusive approach to social science analysis. In most cases, however, analysis was nationally and regionally specific and the level of global conceptualization was limited to 'the West and the rest'. In the era of rapidly expanding development studies, the overwhelming focus of development analysis was on the current post-war era – an implicit assumption that historical trends were of little interest for much of the world.

## Second-generation global social science analysis, from the 1980s

Global studies gathered steam and entered a second generation in the 1980s, as the term 'globalization' came to represent the expansion in

DOI: 10.1057/9781137378972

global economic and cultural interconnections. Datasets created in this second generation of global studies were more explicitly transnational and transdisciplinary, and they were structured in the more flexible and relational technology developed in those years. This was the era of spreadsheets and relational databases. In some cases, large institutions took on research and data display in this updated framework. Among these institutions were Hitotsubashi University (Tokyo), the United Nations Population Division, and a few others (HITOTSUBASHI, UNPOP). Much of the original research in global studies, however, was carried out by individuals and small groups of scholars, whose datasets and analyses therefore risked being neglected rather than integrated into the larger task of global analysis (GEHN). Angus Maddison developed global estimates of population and gross domestic product that were less specific but more extensive, addressing much of the world for the last millennium (Maddison Project).

Academic programs in global studies began to form in U.S. universities. Most of the U.S. National Resource Centers in International Studies adopted the term 'globalization' but continued to focus primarily on international studies and international business in the short term, without significant emphasis on research or long-term analysis. A few programs, however, undertook the research and analysis of the second generation. Two outstanding programs of the second generation are the Institute for Research on World-Systems (IROWS) at the University of California, Riverside and the Earth Institute at Columbia University, which has undertaken major research in natural and social sciences as well as its policy-oriented support of the United Nations Millennium Program on global inequality, although its historical studies are limited to climate (IROWS; EARTH).

With the era of globalization, attention to data on global issues expanded, facilitated by the advances in computer technology, the development of personal computers, and the emergence of practical Global Information Systems (GIS). As a result, the expanded social science datasets of this era gave great attention to spatial designation but not much attention to temporal analysis. The two pioneering projects were the Great American History Machine (GAHM), years ahead of its time in mapping U.S. census and electoral data via a windowing interface, and the joint project between the Newberry Library and the University of Wisconsin Automated Cartography Laboratory which mapped changing U.S. county boundaries (Miller and Modell 1988, Langran 1992). A series

DOI: 10.1057/9781137378972

of European projects followed shortly after, the largest being the Swedish National Topographic Database (Goerke 1994). The Alexandria Digital Library emerged as an impressive gazetteer system (Hill et al. 1999).

Two national historical GIS systems stood out in Britain and the U.S. The Great Britain Historical GIS achieved high performance by holding all statistical metadata in a set of extensively denormalized relational tables, tightly linked to statistical data values held in one column of a single very large table rather than in external text files (Southall et al. 2009). The U.S. National Historical GIS (NHGIS) relied substantially on a large-scale project for defining metadata, the Data Documentation Initiative (Blank and Rasmussen 2004). Both addressed the issue of setting statistics into these spatially focused datasets. In later years the same issue was pursued in the Colonial Legacies Project (which has since become CLIO World Tables), compiling information from global sources into core statistical datasets, creating pools of data coded to administrative reporting units (CLIO; see also Eltis 2010). Despite these advances, there still remain problems in spatial representation of historical data.

Other important projects which developed during this second generation of global studies included the CIDOC Conceptual Reference Model for cultural heritage materials (CIDOC); the system for sampling national census results developed by the Integrated Public Use Microdata Series (IPUMS) for the U.S. and for several other countries; and the Electronic Cultural Atlas Initiative (ECAI).[1] For these as for the geographically focused datasets, the lack of sufficient links of data values to each other through metadata means that they remain principally as repository projects – they raise interest in the possibility of interactive analysis, but they do not themselves enable such analysis. The second generation of global studies, the era of contemporary globalization, advanced to giving explicit attention to global patterns and led to serious efforts at documenting contemporary global patterns. Nevertheless the approach to documenting global patterns focused primarily on reification of contemporary national units – a poor framework for evaluating long-term change.

# Third-generation global social science analysis?

Are we now opening a third generation of global studies? Researchers are nowhere near to having a set of global historical data against which

DOI: 10.1057/9781137378972

to test emerging large-scale theory. Global theory, in turn, remains vague for lack of comprehensive data to explore. The CHIA group, rather than wait for a gradual accretion of localized projects to bring about large-scale analysis, seeks to speed the transition into global social analysis by launching a large-scale initiative. The data, technology, and readiness of researchers to collaborate are within reach; the CHIA collaborative has the experience and the organizational skills, and it now seeks large-scale institutional support. Expansion of the CHIA campaign can decisively address the remaining gap: it can advance global analysis in social sciences by leading in creation of a consolidated system of information and also by resolving many attendant technical and organizational challenges. Whether CHIA remains the sole center for assembling global historical data and analysis or whether it attracts other major groupings and becomes part of a larger collaborative effort, the launching of this collaborative will speed and strengthen the long-overdue process of systematically documenting the human record. If the work expands rapidly enough, CHIA may become a minor portion of the overall project, as major new groups join the effort; if the work expands slowly, it is possible that CHIA will continue to lead.

## Global study of climate: data and modeling

The study of climate proceeded quietly and marginally among small and often dispersed groups of researchers until the techniques for research and the need for research results led to acceleration of climate studies in the post-war era.[2] Efforts to model and predict climate began in the nineteenth century, and in the early twentieth century the British mathematician Lewis Fry Richardson made a serious effort to define and calculate short-term changes in climate, though without success. Only after World War II in the United States, with the computer modeling of John Von Neumann, did efforts to model climate – especially temperature and precipitation – become sustained. Researchers soon learned that they had a better chance of success in modeling small regions, because there was a better chance of getting adequate empirical data on climate with which to verify their results. By the 1960s, efforts at modeling became more diverse: some researchers made simplifications in order to focus in greater detail on space, while others focused on modeling changes over time, on radiation transfer, or on surface effects such as evaporation – the complexity

DOI: 10.1057/9781137378972

of modeling and computation was too great to do all at once, given the technology then available. Another way to address additional complexities was through 'parameterization' – that is, complex phenomena such as clouds or the interactions of waves and winds were approximated not through specification of a dynamic but by adopting a single figure, a parameter, to refer to each such factor.

All of the models that sought to explain climate in terms of a single factor simply failed: it became clear that it would be necessary to posit the interaction of multiple factors and dynamics. Indeed, the advances in modeling brought the successive inclusion of element after element of the earth's geophysical system: the atmosphere, landmasses, the oceans, snow and ice, and the biosphere. In initial steps along this trajectory, it became possible by the 1960s to make valuable weather predictions for as much as three days. These initial benefits were now sufficient to bring in expanded funding. By the 1970s new researchers and research groups joined the effort. Prominent among them was James Hansen of the Goddard Space Center in New York: his modeling of radiation for the atmosphere of Venus provided a method that was applied with success to earth. Similarly, studies of the physics of clouds and the processes of reflection from snow were added into the mix. An overall system of fluid mechanics became successful, despite the difficulty of modeling climate at the poles, because of the particular properties of a spherical fluid system, like that of the earth. Among the groups applying these methods were several in Europe, where post-war recovery in scientific work had become significant by this time. Japanese-born physicists were central to climate modeling from the start.

As the models became stronger, pressure built for the recovery of more empirical data on climate. Indeed, empirical data had begun to show a relatively rapid increase in the proportion of carbon dioxide ($CO_2$) in the atmosphere. Syukoro Manabe began to research the issue, and from 1965 joined a few others in expressing concern that the rise in atmospheric $CO_2$ might bring a rise in temperature – roughly, that a doubling of the proportion of $CO_2$ would bring a rise of about 3 degrees Celsius in average global temperature. This important prediction brought additional attention to the questions of whether it could be verified and, if so, what implications it would have. A major shift in research began in 1969 with the publication of a co-authored paper by Manabe, working on the atmosphere, and Kirk Bryan, working on the oceans. They sought to model the interaction of atmosphere and ocean,

DOI: 10.1057/9781137378972

but had to address the fact that the atmosphere tends to equilibrate in response to changes (such as $CO_2$ expansion) within a matter of weeks, while the ocean requires centuries to adjust to major shifts. Nonetheless, they developed a computational strategy that showed important patterns of the atmosphere-ocean interaction. Their work led to detailed results for certain world spaces by 1975.

By now a research system had developed in which several labs worked on varied but overlapping tasks. Thus, a 1979 meeting at Woods Hole, Massachusetts, compared results of Manabe and Hansen models, and both showed warming as a result of $CO_2$ increase. At the same time, it had become clear that the ocean soaked up much of the increasing $CO_2$ – the result, however, was not to nullify temperature increase, but to delay it. During the 1970s and 1980s work became far more collaborative, and far more focused on collection of data. The study of ice cores began, making it possible to compare the levels of atmospheric $CO_2$ in the past, as they varied with changes in average temperature. More generally, study of the historical antecedents of contemporary climate expanded, along with international collaboration in data collection and sharing.

As the experience of modeling accumulated, two contradictory general rules appeared. First was that simple models can provide substantial insights into complex processes, pointing in the right direction. Second was that many problems were intractable and took extensive study to resolve. One example of the latter was that models of the 1980s predicted warming at a rate greater than the actual rate. The problem turned out to be that the models had neglected the effects of human-generated aerosols from pollution – these aerosols tended to cool the atmosphere. In other results of more careful modeling, studies in the 1990s tried to explain the decline in average temperature from the 1940s through 1960s. Once the models included the effects of declining solar activity during that period, as well as increased aerosols from pollution and higher-than-normal volcanic activity, they were able to account for the empirical records on temperature.

In another type of discrepancy between models and data from the field, recorded temperatures of the ocean showed figures lower than the models. The problem turned out to be with the instrumentation and processing of empirical temperature observations – that is, the models turned out to be more correct. In a similar discovery, the discrepancy between models and reported temperatures for the higher atmosphere turned out be because of insufficient attention to the temperature of the

DOI: 10.1057/9781137378972

measuring devices. The high stratosphere was now shown to be cooling, as predicted in models for years.

As modeling became steadily more comprehensive, the terminology changed. Thus GCM initially stood for 'general circulation model', referring to the atmosphere, but the acronym came later to stand for 'global climate model'. As the effects of ice were added to those of atmosphere and ocean, the term 'Earth System Model' arose. Meanwhile, the system of climatic archives expanded along with the research. The U.S. National Climatic Data Center (NCDC), located in Asheville, North Carolina, became the world's largest climate archive. It developed out of an office based in New Orleans from 1934, which combined in 1951 with the National Weather Records Center formed in Asheville – the center became the National Climatic Data Center in 1993. Meanwhile, major climate archives developed in other parts of the world, so that the World Data Centers for Meteorology came to be located in the United States, Russia, Japan, and China.

Overall, climate modeling and the global historical dataset that goes with it is a remarkable scientific achievement, greatly successful already and doubtless with much additional knowledge to be produced. In public discussion of climate analysis, far more attention has been given to the modeling than to the collection of data used in the models. The data are distributed among many repositories but are called together as needed for calculations.

## Genetics: creating a global dataset

Serious work on molecular genetics could not begin until the genetic code was broken in the 1950s. From that point, an understanding of the molecular basis of genetics led to important breakthroughs in genetic knowledge. DNA molecules were found to be composed of pairs of long strands made up from four amino acids, reproduced with incredible accuracy whenever a cell divided – but the work of determining the specific sequence of any strand of DNA was difficult and slow. By the 1980s, remarkable machines had been developed that minimized waste almost to zero as they sliced the strands and identified the amino acids, one after another. These techniques worked most easily on short strands of DNA, such as those located in the mitochondria, which lie inside each cell but outside the nucleus.

DOI: 10.1057/9781137378972

In a remarkable experiment, a group of molecular biologists at the University of California, Berkeley, sequenced mitochondrial DNA (Mt-DNA) for 147 persons, many living in California but with ancestry from many parts of the world (Cann et al. 1987). Mitochondrial DNA, in addition to being a small molecule, is passed only through the female line, so that it reflects descent from mother to child. This tiny sample nonetheless gave a striking and robust result: the genetic differences among the few African-American subjects were greater than those among all other subjects. Based on the simple assumption that mutation and differentiation of Mt-DNA took place at a constant rate, the differences among the genomes of the subjects were treated as a 'molecular clock', indicating that Europeans, Asians, and Amerindians had only about 50,000 years of separation from each other, while the Africans (even as represented mainly by African-Americans) had differences among themselves that could be traced back 200,000 years.

This experiment, simple at a certain level, was challenged and followed up with many studies accounting for additional complexities. Yet the research confirmed the unity, recent origin, and African homeland of the human species. The conceptual importance of this result, replacing earlier theories of slow differentiation of humans in several parts of the Old World, was the realization that the human species, despite the superficial differences known as 'race', developed recently and expanded suddenly to the limits of the world.

This result brought expansion of research into detailed sequencing of the human genome, plus the sequencing of genomes of many other species. For a time, it seemed that researches would be limited to tracing descent through the female line. The Y chromosome, the male sex-determining chromosome, for years seemed resistant to the sort of analysis that paralleled the analysis of female descent through Mt-DNA, but ultimately yielded a great number of haplotypes (sequences of amino acids in a given range of the genome) enabling the tracing of male lines as they diverged over time.

The step that most clearly crystallized the importance and influence of genetic research was the Human Genome Project. From its creation in 1989 it brought forth unexpected energy, so that it accelerated and reached its target by 2001 (Anon. 2012; Baldi and Hatfield 2002; Anon. 2013). Even with the full genome outlined, however, immense work remained to be done on individual and group variation at many points along the genome.

DOI: 10.1057/9781137378972

As with climate analysis, the results of genetic analysis led to some errors in historical analysis. In fact, the data on DNA all came from the present day – samples from persons living as they provided their evidence. To understand the implications of these samples for the past, one needed to attribute a past population as ancestors of the living samples. Geneticists at first accepted oversimplified assumptions on race and civilization, underestimating the degree to which physical characteristics can change in a population over time. They also underestimated the degree of mixing among families and peoples – or the degree to which a little early mixing could spread characteristics far and wide over time.

But with time, geneticists came to be more sophisticated in their understanding of language and social structure as devices for linking present populations to past populations. As a result, genetic evidence provides evidence not only for the very short term – linking an individual to parents and grandparents – but also for the very long term – giving clear indications on early human origins and migrations. Indeed, genetic evidence is valuable for study of every time frame in between those extremes. In a seeming contradiction, the human genome – as compared with other animal species – exhibits a remarkable unity and overall similarity, yet it also reveals immense variability within the limits of that unity.

As for genetic archives, in one sense, the genetic code of living individuals is an archive from which to explore biological change at any scale – from short-term family-level change to the era of human origins and beyond. In another sense, the archive is the distributed archive of research results held by many individual scholars. The main public archive is GenBank, the National Institutes of Health (NIH) database maintained and distributed by the U.S. National Center for Biotechnology Information (GenBank, NCBI). It stores public DNA sequences submitted from individual scientists and from large centers involved in the Human Genome Project. The public version of GenBank was created in 1982 at Los Alamos National Laboratory, principally by NIH, but with support from the U.S. National Science Foundation, Department of Energy, and Department of Defense.

For genetic data, we commonly hear a great deal more about the empirical results than about modeling to make sense of the data. In fact, modeling of genetic change over time remains a productive yet controversial area of research. For our purposes, however, the key message is that a huge, distributed archive of genetic evidence has been developed

DOI: 10.1057/9781137378972

in just over 20 years. Geneticists are fortunate to have been able to rely on a wonderful system of citation and collection of data – the PubMed system, which indexes and retrieves almost the entire literature in medical and biological sciences (PubMed). It resulted from substantial investment by the U.S. government and the medical and bioscience community. From 1971 to 1997, the MEDLINE online system provided access to the MEDLARS computerized database (compiled by agencies of the U.S. government), which was made available at medical libraries and similar institutions. The succeeding PubMed, system, released in 1997, has since remained free to the public.

For both climatology and genomics, the successes of expanded research, modeling, and data repositories may superficially appear as inevitable progress in knowledge. Even the brief narratives presented above, however, show that the pattern of research development was complex and contingent. At the core was specific, excellent scientific analysis, but that was never enough. Social concerns and public debate on climate and genetics attracted the attention of researchers and generated research funding. The analysis focused on a series of key questions, and involved imaginative use of theory. In each case, new technology was central to the expansion of knowledge. The newly discovered data were both contemporary and historical. At every stage, expansion of knowledge relied on collaboration among groups of researchers. Meanwhile, for both of these large projects, the researchers found their paths slowed and diverted because of skepticism within the scientific community and in society at large.

In climate and genomics, the principal research issue shifted with time – from short-term weather to long-term climate change, and from overall genetic structure to the working of specific genes – with the result that research had to become more comprehensive in its system of research and documentation. Theorists, therefore, needed to be flexible and able to shift their emphasis to new links among theoretical issues. In addition, historical data became essential to solving each of the big problems in climate and genetics. In each case, the need to understand processes of change over time was essential to understanding the dynamics under study. If the analogy holds, the collection of world-historical data on human society might benefit from the sudden recognition of the importance of a research issue (such as the problem of growing economic inequality), or from a sudden technological advance that facilitates global data collection. Government agencies, under such

DOI: 10.1057/9781137378972

circumstances, might conclude that this research deserves public support. Of course the study of world history remains distinct from other fields in many ways. For instance, it requires parallel data from all parts of the world and therefore requires an extraordinary level of collaboration. Overall, this comparative perspective suggests that global analysis in social science is developing more slowly than that in natural science, but only by a few decades. It is possible that social scientific study of the world, past and present, could become, in a few decades, work at a level of intensity and productivity parallel to that in natural science fields.

## A long-term home for CHIA?

What governmental or intergovernmental agency should give the key support to building the CHIA project? As is clear, the U.S. government took the lead and became the principal source of financial support and archival institutions to develop the global and historical analysis of climate and the human genome. In both of these cases, however, the initial U.S. lead came to be supplemented by institutions of international collaboration: parallel centers of research support and archival repositories that are shared by countries with the largest scientific establishments, notably Japan, Russia, China, United Kingdom, and France.

For the world-historical archive, where will it ultimately repose? It seems to me that there are three principal candidates, and an obvious choice among them. The U.S. government remains the largest and best-organized government, and its support of social science research through the National Science Foundation exceeds that from any other institution worldwide. The World Bank, headquartered in Washington, is the principal international economic organization, and has energetically collected worldwide economic statistics for times as early as 1950 (WB). The United Nations Educational, Scientific, and Cultural Organization (UNESCO), headquartered in Paris, is the most representative of international organizations addressing scientific issues, and it serves as headquarters for all the main scientific organizations worldwide. In technological and financial terms, the U.S. government is best equipped to support this work because of the breadth and depth of its resources: its initial support of CHIA through the National Science Foundation reflects this advance. Yet the United States is only one nation among many: it has only 6 per cent of global population and, because of contemporary

DOI: 10.1057/9781137378972

global tensions, is not best placed to achieve the universal collaboration that is necessary for the collection of historical data from every area of the world. The World Bank has substantial resources, a near-universal membership of nations, and has excellent experience around the world in economic research and experience. But it does not have the strength in other areas of social science that would be necessary to support the development of a comprehensive world-historical data resource.

I believe that UNESCO is the best home for CHIA, even though it is known that UNESCO has an inefficient and bureaucratic structure, slowed by political conflicts. The essential nature of CHIA is to collect balanced information on all areas of the world and to link them together effectively in a picture of global change and development. This requires the openness to all regional interests that is the strength of UNESCO. The World Bank could be effective on economic data, but is not a strong institution for the collection of social and natural science data that are fundamentally important in a world-historical data resource, and it is widely regarded as tied principally to powerful economic interests. The U.S. government could do a great deal to support research and to build data resources that would be of essential benefit in getting the global dataset started. But for the dataset to reach its potential, global collaboration must be fundamental. From this perspective, it is unfortunate that the United States has twice withdrawn from UNESCO, and that it has been a non-member of UNESCO for three years as of this writing.

In one sense, CHIA is to be a technical effort, drawing on the historical record to assemble the story of social change at the global level. In another sense, the study of history is rarely regarded as socially or politically neutral. There have been great struggles over the relationship of history to current politics in many nations and for the world as a whole.[3] It is entirely possible that some elements of CHIA will become politically controversial. Yet to have the CHIA Archive placed under the governance of an international organization, with nearly universal membership of the world's nations, would seem to provide a better forum for the debate on historical controversies than if the archive were governed by a single nation.

For these reasons UNESCO presents unique advantages as the ultimate home for the CHIA repository. But we have already learned from the experience with climate and genomics that, in addition to the need for a primary home for such a global archive, international collaboration is essential in maintaining data collections and supporting research.

DOI: 10.1057/9781137378972

For that reason, the World Bank should be invited to work with setting up global datasets in economic life that meet the stringent standards of those proposed for CHIA. And the government of the U.S. – and of other countries with active social science research groups (UK, Canada, Japan, South Korea, and the European Union) should be encouraged to build national-level institutions to support the CHIA project.

To summarize, the comparison of climatic and genetic data analysis with that for world history leads to some clear suggestions, though no clear prediction of how the experience will go. Each of the three fields of scientific analysis developed significantly in conceptual terms during the nineteenth century. In the early twentieth century each field invested expanded effort, but without definitive results. In the second half of the twentieth century, climatology, geology, and biological studies each experienced dramatic advances because of great advances in instrumentation and in theory, and both benefitted from advances in computing power. Social sciences developed as well, but not because of instrumentation and not in the direction of overall reconceptualization – in fact social sciences became more specific rather than more general in their analysis.

Over the longer term, however, the differences between these fields and between these research efforts appear to diminish. While climatology began with theory and genetics began with empirical work, both relied heavily on laboratory work, both ended up with an interplay of theory and empirical work, and both relied heavily on historical data. Similarly, while study of human society has focused overwhelmingly on communities and nations and on small-scale theories, there is an indication now that both historical data and broad theorization may grow.

In climatology, analysis focused first on weather forecasting and then shifted to focus on growth in $CO_2$; in the course of this change many other specializations in climatology developed. In genetics, work focused first on basic genetic dynamics then shifted to tracing of species development and then to current medical treatment. For social sciences, concerns with economic growth and governance have tended to predominate in the last two decades, but it may be that the discovery of new dynamics in social processes will lead research in unexpected directions. Thus, while it is surely important that each research project be hypothesis-driven – intended to bring back relevant results – it is equally important to keep an eye on the possibility that advances in research on human society may open up crucial new problems to solve, for which

DOI: 10.1057/9781137378972

research previously thought to be marginal sometimes turns out to have central importance. Meanwhile, further bases for consideration and comparison of climatology, genomics, and historical studies of human society must surely be the handling of data – documentation, storage, and availability – and the maximization of open communication among scholars working in the field.

Contemporary social science focuses overwhelmingly on nations as spatial units of analysis and on governance and economic growth or decline as the key issues for study. The primacy of this research focus is surely relative rather than absolute. The human experience definitely depends heavily on spatial units of a scale different from that of nations (this indeed is suggested by the range in the size of nations), and the accelerating changes in global ecology will make clear that it is necessary to analyze territorial units that are ecologically rather than politically defined. The shifting perspectives within climatology and genomics provide a clear hint that flexibility and multiplicity in analytical approaches is the way for social scientists to go in their alliances with each other and with scholars in humanities, natural sciences, and information sciences.

## Notes

1   And, for the natural science community, the World Data System (WDS) of the International Council for Science (ICSU).
2   This account of the effort to model and document global climate relies principally on Weart 2008.
3   At the global level, Huntington (1996) made the controversial argument that a millennium of conflict between Christianity and Islam had defined contending Christian and Islamic worlds which would remain in conflict. At the national level, in Japan the controversy continues over politicians' visits to the Yasukuni Shrine and the related question of Japanese apologies for acts carried out during World War II.

DOI: 10.1057/9781137378972

# 8

# Priorities for CHIA; Benefits of CHIA

Abstract: *The CHIA project, still in its early stages, already includes some 25 activities in infrastructure building and data collection. The task of coordinating these collaborative projects becomes more complex with time, but success in collection of data, development of applications to assist in data collection, and even the early interpretive results of this work are already providing encouragement to stay at work. We will learn, for instance, whether long-term cycles of social inequality have long prevailed or whether they are a development of our own age. CHIA's top priorities, at present, are to focus on the global framework, expand the crowdsourcing application, collect historical data worldwide, expand peer reviewing of datasets, and explore cross-disciplinary theory. Additional priorities are proposed for subsequent work.*

Keywords: priorities

Manning, Patrick. *Big Data in History*. Basingstoke: Palgrave Macmillan, 2013. DOI: 10.1057/9781137378972.

The priorities for CHIA during its initial five-year campaign, as expressed in Chapter 3, have been debated and revised, with the result that they have developed by stages in logic and coherence. In practice, however, they will doubtless need to be revisited many times in order to address the many choices and possible courses of action facing those who are executing the overall plan. We face the recurring question: what priorities should CHIA set among its many possible courses of action? The list of tasks identified throughout this text is daunting. Yet these are the tasks that, arguably, need to be completed in order to create a substantial and successful data resource, one that that models the principal processes in human society over the past several centuries. Even if the project were amply funded, one can see that inadequate management might lead it to run out of resources or lose track of the key issues and end up with little to show for an immense expenditure of energy. So it is very important to prioritize tasks for CHIA that are central and productive.

Here is an initial suggestion of top priorities for work in the next few years. Each of these priority steps is at once *necessary*, in that the project must complete it in order to continue, and *sufficient*, in that it will bring benefits not only to CHIA but to social science analysis and cross-disciplinary work in general.

1    **Global repository, global analysis.** CHIA must maintain its objective of designing a big but extendable data repository in order to avoid distractions and make the best choices in development of this global resource. The CHIA Archive will preserve and display all datasets submitted, along with the transformed and aggregated data. The benefit for social sciences will be a systematic effort to clarify global perspectives.

2    **Crowdsourcing for data collection and documentation.** This infrastructure must create a feasible and attractive option for those ready to submit and document data for a comprehensive repository. It will benefit social science in developing collaborative practice. The infrastructure requires seamless clarity in the interface, energetic staff support, and tutorials enabling users to develop the skills to contribute their data effectively and continue with the process of integrating the data into the CHIA Archive. The integrated data are to include a full set of metadata in spatial, temporal, topical, and source terms.

DOI: 10.1057/9781137378972

3   **Effective collection of historical data worldwide.** Collection of
    numerous datasets will expand the ability of the CHIA archive
    to identify global historical patterns. For social science, the
    development of global historical data will lead to new analytical
    insights. Yet researchers and institutions have many reasons for
    not contributing data: the data are not yet fully processed, they
    are kept private while a publication is being prepared, the cost
    of duplicating and transferring the data, the hope for profit from
    providing the data, and the simple unwillingness to give up control
    of valuable data. All of these are understandable, but in total they
    do not offset the tremendous value of data on the human past for
    the understanding of processes of social change. The CHIA project
    must effectively encourage professional and amateur historians to
    gather and submit data of world-historical relevance; CHIA must
    analyze and visualize the developing results.

4   **Peer reviewing of historical datasets.** The peer reviewing of
    datasets, notably in the *Journal of World-Historical Information*, will
    bring scholarly critique of datasets and maintain high standards
    and best practices. The benefit for social science is to give
    recognition to the value of creating and publishing historical data.
    At present, the emphasis within social sciences and humanities
    privileging monographic interpretation downplays the actual
    handling of existing data, as with translations and annotations, and
    the creation of new datasets assembles from primary documents.
    The advance of social science scholarship in general requires more
    attention to identifying and rewarding examples of high-level
    preparation of data; the development of world-historical analysis
    requires such advance in best practices all the more because it must
    stretch across temporal, spatial, and socio-cultural boundaries.
    JWHI and other journals must expand solicitation and publication
    of dataset reviews.

5   **Cross-disciplinary theory.** Theoretical study will address
    interconnection at micro and macro levels to show interactions
    across disciplines and will facilitate estimation of missing data and
    linking of variables. The benefit for social sciences is the further
    emphasis on macro-theorization and disciplinary interplay. In
    the context of global analysis, the varying realms of social science
    theory will be able gradually to nurture relationships with each
    other. Interdisciplinary conferences, aimed at developing global

DOI: 10.1057/9781137378972

data, will assist in this regard: the Global Historical Population conference (Amsterdam, October 2013) is an example.[1]

These five top priorities apply to the initial several years of the CHIA project, calendar years 2013–17.[2] For each of these objectives, we already have insights and resources that point us in the direction of achieving the goal. Yet there remain major problems that we have only begun to address. One of these is the high cost (in time and money) of data collection and digitization of historical data. The initial CHIA repository can hope to provide a valuable sample of world-historical data – enough to launch major new initiatives of research and interpretation. But to confirm the global hypotheses that will arise from initial investigation, it will be necessary to continue at length in research, digitization, harmonization, and aggregation of data on the human past. The funds necessary for historical research and indeed for training of skilled historians are not available now. One may hope that the initial results of world-historical analysis will show the value of such work, and will lead to additional support for its continuation. A second unsolved problem is that of intellectual property. The complex transformation, aggregation, and distribution of data through the CHIA archive will increase the difficulty of retaining and conveying the identity of the sources, compilers, and developers of the data at every level; yet the maintenance of a clear record of each step in data manipulation is necessary to preserve data integrity and to make necessary updates. This dilemma will require concentrated attention at every stage of work.

For the projected second five years of the CHIA project (2018–22), the following major priorities, if pursued successfully, should lead the project to becoming a fully established archive, ready for a longer-term process of maintenance and gradual expansion.

1  Collect additional historical data, with special emphasis on under-documented times, places, and topics. This work should include estimation of missing values to permit creation of relatively complete global and regional data series.
2  Develop an institutional system enabling researchers to prepare and submit a continuing stream of additional historical data.
3  Advance the techniques for interdisciplinary analysis of historical data, to extract a wider range of interpretive results from the growing archive.

DOI: 10.1057/9781137378972

4   Disseminate the CHIA archive and its resources to researchers, teachers, and students worldwide.

5   Establish an institutional home: a lasting relationship with an international organization that will provide funding and administrative support to maintain the archive and enable it to develop to its potential.

## Can readers help to build a world-historical archive?

While the task of developing world-historical data remains daunting, we can already see glimmers of the patterns that may be documented and explained in the years to come. As usual, one turns to studies of climate to begin this list of examples. The phenomenon known as El Niño Southern Oscillation (ENSO), which brings alternating periods of wet and dry weather to opposite shores of the southern Pacific Ocean, began to be studied seriously only in the 1970s. By now, however, El Niño episodes have been documented in timing and intensity for the past several hundred years. In studies of human population, we have detailed worldwide documentation only for the last half century; documentation for earlier times is restricted to a few highly literate regions. Yet with the techniques now available, it will be possible to estimate rates of birth, death, and migration around the world to give new and improved estimates of past population and population change, so that we can hope for valuable estimates of world population during the past four centuries with just a few years of additional research. And, to add one more example that is at once more specific and of wide interest, we have the hope of preparing detailed estimates of the flows of silver from mines (especially in Mexico and Bolivia) to purchasers and users worldwide for the past four centuries. Silver became the principal form of liquid wealth around the world from about 1600: by tracing the quantities of its production and its flows around world regions, we will gain new insights into money supplies, commercial transactions, financial fluctuations, and the economic linkages among regional economies.

The two principal ways in which readers of this book can help to build a world-historical archive are to contribute directly to construction of the archive and to develop world-historical thinking more generally. Throughout the book I have emphasized the first of these – the ways in

DOI: 10.1057/9781137378972

which contributors and users can provide datasets, work directly or indirectly with project staff to develop the CHIA infrastructure, and explore the CHIA Archive to seek out the historical relationships that it reveals. Here I conclude by emphasizing the benefits that individuals and groups can bring about simply by asking global questions and looking for global relationships.

Questions about silver and El Niño have already been mentioned; here are some more. Literacy has expanded steadily over many centuries, but in the last half-century we suddenly reached the point where the majority of the adult population is literate: what difference does that make for human society and communication? How and why has the nature of work shifted so much from century to century? For instance, why did slavery expand to so much of the world from the seventeenth through the nineteenth centuries? Why did child labor rise and decline – or did it really decline? How did the expansion of steam shipping change relations among world regions? Did transportation affect the rise of nationhood? Have war and violence increased or declined with time? How did family life change with patterns of migration, climate change, or governance? Why have new diseases, both infectious and chronic, appeared in each new phase of human development? What types of new diseases await us at the next stage? As noted earlier, these questions can be posed for one factor at a time, for the interaction of multiple factors, and to account for the dynamics of spatial interaction, change over time, and scales from local to global.[3]

If the number of questions about global historical patterns expands, there will be more attention to CHIA and to other resources on our global past from students, teachers, researchers, and policymakers. Each will be asking where she or he fits into global society. Each will develop a sense of where social problems are being solved and where new problems are arising. And each will get an improved sense of the rates of change in various arenas of human society: where change is rapid (perhaps in fashion), where change is slow (as in the character of family relations), and where it is cyclical (as in cycles of prosperity and depression).

A broad discussion in many parts of the world will set the present era in the context of the past and will encourage people at all levels of society to participate in retrieving and reconsidering the evidence available on past social change. The results will enrich our lives in any case because of the many fascinating stories to be retrieved from the past, and they will provide us with a better sense of the gradual trajectory or trajectories

DOI: 10.1057/9781137378972

of human society – the long-term developments that influence our lives from generation to generation as well as the short-term developments that dominate our daily existence.

# Notes

1   This small conference (25–26 October 2013) was co-sponsored by the World History Center, University of Pittsburgh, and CLIO-INFRA, at the International Institute of Social History, Amsterdam.
2   The reader may wish to compare this set of overall CHIA priorities with the earlier list of priorities in developing project infrastructure: see Chapter 3. The previous list has been compressed as follows: Global collaboration (collaboration, CHIA archive, digital stewardship); crowdsourcing (ingest, integration, gazetteer, temporal search engine, ontology); peer review; data collection; and theory.
3   See Chapter 2.

DOI: 10.1057/9781137378972

# References

References are shown in two sections: in Organizations, with organizational name and website organized alphabetically by acronym or short name; and in Bibliography, with books and articles organized alphabetically by author surname.

## Organizations

▶

CHIA. Collaborative for Historical Information and Analysis (http://www.chia.pitt.edu).

ChronoZoom. ChronoZoom (http://www.chronozoom.com/).

CIDOC. International Committee for Documentation, International Council for Museums (http://www.cidoc-crm.org/index.html).

CLACSO. Consejo Latinoamericano de Ciencias Sociales, Buenos Aires (http://www.clacso.org.ar).

CLIO. CLIO World Tables (http://blogs.bu.edu/jgerring/files/2013/06/ColonialismLegacies.pdf).

CLIO-INFRA. Clio Infrastructure, supported by the European Commission initiative Digital Research Infrastructure for the Arts and Humanities (http://www.clio-infra.eu).

CODESRIA. Council for the Development of Economic and Social Research in Africa, Dakar (http://www.codesria.org).

DOI: 10.1057/9781137378972

DCMI. Dublin Core Metadata Initiative, Association for Information Science and Technology (http://dublincore.org).

DDI. Data Documentation Initiative, DDI Alliance (http://www.ddialliance.org).

DVN. The Dataverse Network, Institute for Quantitative Social Science, Harvard University (http://thedata.org).

EARTH. Earth Institute, Columbia University (http://www.earth.columbia.edu/).

ECAI. Electronic Cultural Atlas Initiative, University of California – Berkeley (http://www.ecai.org).

GALAXY ZOO. Galaxy Zoo, a project of Zooinverse, Citizen Science Alliance (http://www.galaxyzoo.org/).

Gapminder. Gapminder Foundation, Stockholm (http://www.gapminder.org)

GBHGIS. Great Britain Historical GIS (http://www.port.ac.uk/research/gbhgis/). See also A Vision of Britain through Time (http:// www.visionofbritain.org.uk).

GCHLR. Global Collaboratory on the History of Labour Relations, International Institute of Social History, (https://collab.iisg.nl/web/labourrelations).

GEHN. Global Economic History Network, London School of Economics, (http://www.lse.ac.uk/economichistory/Research/GEHN/Home.aspx).

GenBank. GenBank, the National Institutes of Health genetic sequence database (http://www.ncbi.nlm.nih.gov/genbank/).

HITOTSUBASHI. Hitotsubashi University (Tokyo) (http://www.hit-u.ac.jp/laboratories/index-e.html).

HRAF. Human Relations Area Files, Yale University. (http://www.yale.edu/hraf/). Established in 1949.

ICPSR. Interuniversity Consortium on Political and Social Research, University of Michigan (http://www.icpsr.umich.edu/).

IPUMS. Integrated Public Use Microdata Series, Minnesota Population Center (http://www.ipums.org).

IQSS. Institute for Quantitative Social Science, Harvard University (http://www.iq.harvard.edu).

IROWS. Institute for Research on World Systems, University of California – Riverside (http://www.irows.ucr.edu).

Linked Data. Site administered by Tom Heath on behalf of the LinkedData community (http://linkeddata.org).

DOI: 10.1057/9781137378972

Maddison Project. Maddison Project, to pursue the measurement of historical economic performance by the late Angus Maddison (http://www.ggdc.net).

MPC. Minnesota Population Center, University of Minnesota (http://www.pop.umn.edu/).

NBER. U.S. National Bureau of Economic Research (http://www.nber.org/data/).

NCBI. National Center for Biotechnology Information (http://www.ncbi.nlm.nih.gov).

NDSA. National Digital Stewardship Alliance (http://www.digitalpreservation.gov/ndsa/).

NHGIS. National Historical Geographic Information System, Minnesota Population Center (www.nhgis.org);

OECD. Organization of Economic Cooperation and Development, Paris (http://www.oecd.org/statistics/).

PastPlace. PastPlace API providing access to information from A Vision of Britain through Time (http://www.programmableweb.com/api/pastplace).

Project Tycho™. Project TYCHO, University of Pittsburgh (http://www.tycho.pitt.edu/).

PSC. Pittsburgh Supercomputing Center (http://www.psc.edu).

PTVM. Periodic Table of Visualization Methods, Visual Literacy, University St. Gallen (http://www.visual-literacy.org/periodic_table/periodic_table.html).

PubMed. National Center for Biotechnology Information (http://www.ncbi.nlm.nih.gov/pubmed).

Sound Toll. Sound Toll records, University of Groningen (http://www.soundtoll.nl). These are the shipping records of the Sound Toll at the entrance to the Baltic Sea.

TED. Technology, Entertainment, Design; Ted Conferences LLC (http://www.ted.com).

Terra Populus. Terra Populus: Integrated Data on Population and Environment, Minnesota Population Center (http://www.terrapop.org/).

Tombouctou Manuscripts Project. Tombouctou Manuscripts Project, University of Cape Town (http://www.tombouctoumanuscripts.org).

UN. United Nations (http://un.org). For United Nations data, see http://data.un.org/Explorer.aspx.

DOI: 10.1057/9781137378972

UNESCO. United Nations Educational, Social, and Cultural Organization (http://www.unesco.org). For UNESCO data, see http://stats.uis.unesco.org.

UNPOP. United Nations Population Division (http://www.un.org/esa/population/unpop.htm).

WB. World Bank, Washington, DC (http://data.worldbank.org/).

WDS. World Data System of the International Commission of Science (http://www.icsu-wds.org/).

WHC. World History Center, University of Pittsburgh (http://www.worldhistory.pitt.edu).

WHD. World-Historical Dataverse: the University of Pittsburgh affiliate of CHIA, housed in the World History Center. (http://www.dataverse.pitt.edu).

WorldMap. WorldMap, Center for Geographic Analysis, Harvard University (http://worldmap.harvard.edu).

XSEDE. Extreme Science and Engineering Discovery Environment, National Center for Supercomputing Applications, University of Illinois, Champaign-Urbana (http://www.xsede.org).

# Bibliography

Anon. 2012. 'A Brief History of the Human Genome Project'. http://www.genome.gov/12011239.

Anon. 2013. 'Major Events in the U.S. Human Genome Project and Related Projects'. http://web.ornl.gov/sci/techresources/Human_Genome/project/timeline.shtml; see also http://www.ornl.gov/hgmis.

Atwell, William. 2001. 'Volcanism and Short-Term Climatic Change in East Asian and World History, c. 1200–1699'. *Journal of World History* 12:29–98.

Bain, D. J., and G. S. Brush. 2008. 'Gradients, Property Templates, and Land Use Change'. *Professional Geographer* 60(2):224–37.

Baldi, Pierre, and G. Wesley Hatfield. 2002. 'A Brief History of Genomics'. In Baldi and Hatfield, *DNA Microarrays and Gene Expression: From Experiments to Data Analysis and Modeling* (Cambridge: Cambridge University Press), pp. 1–6.

Bowker, Geoffrey. 2008. *Memory Practices in the Sciences (Inside Technology)*. Cambridge: MIT Press.

DOI: 10.1057/9781137378972

Benton, Lauren. 2002. *Law and Colonial Cultures: Legal Regimes in World History, 1400–1900.* New York: Cambridge University Press.

Calhoun, Craig, and Troy Duster. 2005. 'Sociology's Visions and Divisions'. *Chronicle of Higher Education* 51(49): B7.

Cann, R. L., Mark Stoneking, and Allan C. Wilson. 1987. 'Mitochondrial DNA and Human Evolution.' *Nature* 325:31–6.

Chase-Dunn, Christopher, and Salvatore Babones, eds. 2006. *Global Social Change: Historical and Comparative Perspectives.* Baltimore: Johns Hopkins University Press.

Comte, Auguste. 1975. *Cours de Philosophie Positive.* 2 vols. Paris: Hermann.

Cushman, Gregory T. 2003. 'Who Discovered the El Niño-Southern Oscillation? Presidential Symposium on the History of the Atmospheric Sciences: People, Discoveries, and Technologies'. https://ams.confex.com/ams/annual2003/techprogram/paper_58909.htm.

Eltis, David. 1979. 'The Direction and Fluctuation of the Transatlantic Slave Trade, 1821–1843: A Revision of the 1845 Parliamentary Paper'. In Henry A. Gemery and Jan S. Hogendorn, eds, *The Uncommon Market: Essays in the Economic History of the Atlantic Slave Trade* (New York: Academic Press), pp. 273–301.

Eltis, David, Halbert, M. et al. 2010. 'Voyages: The Trans-Atlantic Slave Trade Database'. http://www.slavevoyages.org/

Etzioni, A. 2011. 'Behavioural Economics: Next Steps'. *Journal of Consumer Policy* 34(3): 277–87.

Fogel, Robert William, and Stanley L. Engerman. 1974. *Time on the Cross: The Economics of American Negro Slavery.* Boston: Little Brown.

Gerring, John, Philip Bond, William Barndt, and Carola Moreno. 2005. 'Democracy and Growth: A Historical Perspective'. *World Politics* 57: 323–64.

Giddens, Anthony. 2003. *Runaway World: How Globalization in Reshaping our Lives,* 2nd edn. New York: Routledge.

Goerke, M., ed. 1994. *Coordinates for Historical Maps.* Göttingen: Max-Planck-Institut für Geschichte.

Hill, Linda L., James Frew, and Qi Zheng. 1999. 'Geographic Names: The Implementation of a Gazetteer in a Georeferenced Digital Library'. *D-Lib Magazine* 5(1), DOI: 10.1045/january99-hill.

DOI: 10.1057/9781137378972

Honaker, James, and Gary King. 2010. 'What to do About Missing Values in Time Series Cross-Section Data'. *American Journal of Political Science* 54(2):561–81.

Huntington, Samuel P. 1996. *The Clash of Civilizations and the Remaking of World Order*. New York: Simon and Schuster.

Huxley, Julian. 1946. *UNESCO, Its Purpose and Its Philosophy*. London: UNESCO.

Langran, G. 1992. *Time in Geographic Information Systems*. London: Taylor & Francis.

Manning, Patrick, ed. 1996. *Slave Trades, 1500–1800: Globalization of Forced Labour*. Aldershot, Great Britain, Variorum.

Manning, Patrick. 2003. *Navigating World History: Historians Create a Global Past*. New York: Palgrave Macmillan.

Manning, Patrick. 2010. 'African Population: Projections, 1851–1961'. In Karl Ittmann, Dennis D. Cordell, and Gregory Maddox, eds, *The Demographics of Empire: The Colonial Order and the Creation of Knowledge* (Athens, OH: Ohio University Press), pp. 245–75.

Manning, Patrick. 2013. 'Why Humanity Needs a Global Archive'. http:// www.chia.pitt.edu/about/GlobalArchive.pdf.

Manning, Patrick, and Sanjana Ravi. 2013. 'Cross-Disciplinary Theory in Construction of a World-Historical Archive'. *Journal of World-Historical Information* 1:15–39, DOI 10.5195/jwhi.2013.3.

Manning, Patrick, and Scott Nickleach. Forthcoming . *African Population, 1650–1950: The Eras of Enslavement and Colonial Rule*.

Marx, Karl. 1967. *Capital: A Critique of Political Economy*, 3 vols. ed. Frederick Engels. New York: International Publishers.

McKeown, Adam. 2004. 'Global Migration, 1846–1940'. *Journal of World History* 15:155–89.

Miller, D. and Modell J. 1988. 'Teaching United States history with the Great American History Machine'. *Historical Methods* 21:121–34.

Mitchell, B. R. 2003. *International Historical Statistics: Africa, Asia and Oceania, 1750–2000*, 4th edn. Basingstoke and New York: Palgrave Macmillan.

Mukherjee, Rila, ed. 2011. *Networks in the First Global Age, 1400 – 1800*. New Delhi: Primus Books.

O'Brien, Patrick K. 2006. 'Historiographical Traditions and Modern Imperatives for the Restoration of Global History'. *Journal of Global History* 1:3–39.

DOI: 10.1057/9781137378972

Owens, J. B. 2007. 'Toward a Geographically-Integrated, Connected World History: Employing Geographic Information Systems (GIS)'. *History Compass* 5(6):2014–40.

Pomeranz, Kenneth. 2000. *The Great Divergence: China, Europe, and the Making of the Modern World Economy.* Princeton: Princeton University Press.

Preston, Samuel , Patrick Heuveline, and Michel Guillot. 2000. *Demography: Measuring and Modeling Population Processes.* Hoboken, NJ: Wiley-Blackwell.

Reinhart, Carmen M., and Kenneth Rogoff. 2009. *This Time Is Different: Eight Centuries of Financial Folly.* Princeton: Princeton University Press.

Santayana, George. 1905–06. *The Life of Reason, Or, the Phases of Human Progress.* New York: Charles Scribner's Sons.

Southall, H. 2011. 'Rebuilding the Great Britain Historical GIS, Part 1: Building an Indefinitely Scalable Statistical Database'. *Historical Methods: A Journal of Quantitative and Interdisciplinary History* 44(3):149–59.

Southall, Humphrey, Von Luenen, Alexander, and Aucott, Paula. 2009. 'On the Organisation of Geographical Knowledge: Data Models for Gazetteers and Historical GIS'. In: *E-Science Workshops*, 2009 5th IEEE International Conference on IEEE (Oxford: ), pp. 162–66.

Van Panhuis,Willem G., John Grefenstette, Su Yon Jung, Nian Shong Chok, Anne Cross, Heather Eng, Bruce Y Lee, Vladimir Zadorozhny, Shawn Brown, Derek Cummings, and Donald S. Burke. In press 2013. 'A Century of Infectious Disease Surveillance and Control in the United States.' *New England Journal of Medicine.*

Wallerstein, Immanuel. 2001. *Unthinking Social Science: the Limits of Nineteenth-Century Paradigms.* Philadelphia: Temple University Press.

Weart, Spencer. 2013. 'The Discovery of Global Warming'. http://www.aip.org/history/climate/index.htm.

Zadorozhny, V., L. Raschid, A. Gal. 2008. 'Scalable Catalog Infrastructure for Managing Access Costs and Source Selection in Wide Area Networks'. *International Journal of Cooperative Information Systems*,17, 1. http://www.worldscinet.com/ijcis/17/1701/S0218843008001786.html.

DOI: 10.1057/9781137378972

Zadorozhny, V., P. Manning, D. J. Bain, and R. Mostern. 2013. 'Collaborative for Historical Information and Analysis: Vision and Work Plan'. *Journal of World-Historical Information* 1:1–14.

Zimmer S. M., D. S. Burke. 2009. 'Historical Perspective—Emergence of Influenza A(H1N1) Viruses'. *N Engl J Med* July 16, 361(3):279–85.

DOI: 10.1057/9781137378972

# Index

DOI: 10.1057/9781137378972

DOI: 10.1057/9781137378972

DOI: 10.1057/9781137378972

DOI: 10.1057/9781137378972

Lightning Source UK Ltd.
Milton Keynes UK
UKHW03n0730270418
321742UK00009B/375/P